JESUS IN INDIA: KING OF WISDOM

THE MAKING OF THE FILM & NEW FINDINGS ON JESUS' LOST YEARS

EDWARD T. MARTIN

FOREWORD, AFTERWORD & PHOTOGRAPHS
BY PAUL DAVIDS

YELLOW HAT PUBLISHING
A DIVISION OF YELLOW HAT PRODUCTIONS, INC.
5190 NEIL RD., SUITE #430
RENO, NEVADA 89502
WWW.JESUS-IN-INDIA-THE-MOVIE.COM

Jesus in India: King of Wisdom
The Making of the Film & New Findings on Jesus' Lost Years

Inquiries regarding this book and other Edward T. Martin books about Jesus in India should be addressed to info@jesus-in-india-the-movie.com or to:

YELLOW HAT PUBLISHING
5190 Neil Road, Suite 430, Reno, Nevada 89502

PUBLISHED IN ASSOCIATION WITH JONAH PUBLISHING COMPANY

First Edition
First Printing October 2008

Edited by Paul Davids
Cover design by Jordan Duvall
Foreword, Afterword & Photographs by Paul Davids
Book Cover Adapted from Poster of the movie:
Jesus in India poster © 2008 by Yellow Hat Productions, Inc.
Text excerpts from "Jesus in India" the Movie used with permission

Library of Congress Cataloging in Publication Data for 1st Edition

Martin, Edward T., 1949–
Jesus in India: King of Wisdom – The Making of the Film & New Findings on Jesus' Lost Years
Edward T. Martin — 1st ed.
    p. cm.
Includes bibliography
  1. India — Description, Travel, History, Folklore, Spirituality. 2. Jesus Christ — Miscellanea. 3. "Jesus in India" the Movie 4. Martin, Edward T. 1949– I. Title.

ISBN # 978-0-9819-2444-1
Printed in the United States of America

"India is not just geography or history. It is not only a nation, a country, a mere piece of land. It is something more: it is a metaphor, poetry, something invisible but very tangible. It is vibrating with certain energy fields which no other country can claim..."

---OSHO

from **India My Love, Fragments of a Golden Past**

DEDICATION

This book is dedicated to a courageous, adventurous, and free-thinking group of travelers and researchers who have dared to question authority and ask new questions about the subject of Jesus in India. Among those are:

> *Aziz Kashmiri*
> *Dr. James W. Deardorff*
> *Suzanne Olsson*
> *Arif Khan*
> *Holger Kersten*
> *Prof. Fida Hassnain*
> *Nicolas Notovitch*
> *Swami Abhedananda*
> *Nicholas Roerich*
> *Madame Elisabeth Caspari*
> *Hazrat Mirza Ghulam Ahmad*
> *and many others...*

and to Paul Davids
who had the courage and foresight to
undertake producing and directing the film
"Jesus in India"

Many thanks to my parents, Tommie and Dorothy Martin, whose memory remains evergreen. Many thanks also to film producer/director Paul Davids, who had the vision and courage to go forward with our filming project. Thank you to Paul's wife, Hollace, for being supportive of our project. Special thanks to Robert Rotstan, Jr. for introducing me to Paul Davids and believing in the importance of our project, and to Paul and Hollace's daughter, Jordan Duvall, who designed the cover of this book and the new edition of my previous book about this research, entitled **King of Travelers: Jesus' Lost Years in India.** Thanks also to Jordan for designing the poster of our film, **"Jesus in India."**

Thank you to Anil Kumar Urmil for much hard work and for working with Paul Davids as producer and editor of our film, and also many thanks to Nelvan Thomas Binny, H. R. Madhusudan, Dnyanesh Moghe, Rajneesh Charan and Rajesh Parida. We were a great team! Also, thank you to Sanjay Shetye, our marvelous associate producer and travel agent in India who got us out of many tight spots! A very special thank you to Dr. James Deardorff and to Robert Rotstan, Jr., for his generous involvement and support. Thanks also to Suzanne Olsson and Arif Khan, webmaster of www.tombofjesus.com. Thanks to Helen Billings and Barbara Lamb for their encouragement and wise advice. Also thanks to Father Baptiste, Aziz Kashmiri, the Shankaracharya of Puri and many other people, who appeared both in front of the camera and behind the scenes in India, America and Europe who made our film possible.

Fortean Times cover by Alexander Tomlinson with Jesus portrayal inspired by Hindu deity Shiva, featuring an article on Jesus in India

FOREWORD

By Paul Davids

The film that this book describes was chosen by the Sundance Channel for a national U.S. television broadcast as its Christmas documentary for 2008, with a prime time airing December 22nd and a repeat broadcast the day after Christmas and on the day of New Year's Eve. Additionally, the International Television Division of NBC Universal offers the film for broadcasts around the world.

This is both wonderful and remarkable, because **"Jesus in India"** is admittedly a controversial film. However, we are privileged to live (especially in the United States) in an era when controversy has become a virtue, and debate and the clash of ideas has emerged as a time-honored tradition.

People no longer hide from ideas. If they don't like them, they chew them up, spit them out, stomp on them, shout about them and then move on to other ideas. But sometimes ideas plant a seed, take hold and blossom, re-shaping both popular and traditional culture.

The verdict is not yet in for **"Jesus in India"** as a concept and theory and new direction in religious thought. But if you fail to accept the challenge of considering it, you will be depriving yourself of knowledge of an extraordinary puzzle. This remarkable puzzle, which involves eighteen lost years or "Hidden Years" in the life of Jesus, may well turn out to be a cornerstone for understanding many enigmas about Christianity – like the long-ignored missing but somehow obvious clue in a mystery that remains unsolved. Or perhaps somehow it will eventually be proven a dead end by indisputable dating of documents, DNA testing and other scientific tests and tools. Either way, none of us will be the worse for the truly incredible journey to inquire and discover.

New concepts of the actual, historic person of Jesus of Nazareth are emerging from historic studies of texts discovered since the 1940's in the Holy Land and Egypt, including the ancient gospels of the so-called Gnostic Christians that were found in Nag Hammadi, Egypt.

Even Pope Benedict the 16th has written a book called *Jesus of Nazareth* which acknowledges evolving understandings of the life and meaning of Jesus based on new findings in the modern era.

However, what the Pope does not talk about, which you will learn much about here, is that there is purportedly one particular ancient text about Jesus, long believed to have been seen and studied by a few select scholars and explorers at the Hemis Monastery in Ladakh, India, high in the Himalayas. This text may tell us true things about the Missing Years in the life of the historic Jesus not described in the New Testament and has been translated from Tibetan at least twice.

The questions today are: where is the Tibetan version, and where is the most ancient version of it, purportedly originally written in the Pali language, and how old is it, really?

Does it, as it purports, fill in actual and accurate details of the life of young Jesus, between the ages of twelve and thirty, that are missing from the New Testament?

The author of the book you are about to read is Edward T. Martin, who has long had the wish – his greatest wish – to hold in his hands the manuscript said to exist at the Hemis Monastery at 14,000 foot elevation, near Tibet.

Edward Martin is by any definition an adventurer who has visited almost sixty countries and climbed about a dozen mountains. He is an English teacher from Lampasas, Texas, where he was raised as a member of the Church of Christ but ran afoul of popular opinion in the church organization. The offense he committed was that as a young Bible student he noticed one omission in the New Testament – those Missing Years -- that he thought to be rather serious, and he began asking far too many questions for those in his small town.

Edward T. Martin's first book, **King of Travelers: Jesus' Lost Years in India**, inspired our film **"Jesus in India."** A revised and updated version has recently been published by Yellow Hat Publishing and is available at www.jesus-in-india-the-movie.com and from New Leaf Distributing Company and other sources as well. It will jolt you and challenge much of what you have always taken for granted about the origins of Christianity, but it is not a prerequisite for reading this book.

This book is the story of an adventure in which I participated as a film producer and director, traveling with Edward T. Martin and producer Anil Kumar Urmil and a dedicated crew of Hindus, Muslims, and Christians over 4000 miles in India in search of answers to ancient mysteries. I then continued traveling to continue filming in several other countries, including Italy, the United Kingdom and the United States.

In India, we confronted all kinds of dangers, from terrorism to inhospitable climates, floods, impassable roads and arduous train travel during India's summer monsoon, which was like being roasted alive in an oven. (You'll find that Ed makes many references to the excessive heat during our travels.) But we diligently searched for the answers to the Biblical questions that have robbed Edward T. Martin of many nights of sleep in his five decades of life.

Not only has Ed Martin pointed out many times that information about Jesus between ages twelve and thirty is missing from the New Testament, but two prominent Catholic scholars whom I interviewed at Georgetown University confirmed it as well. Both Professor Alan C. Mitchell and Professor Anthony Tambasco, of the Georgetown Department of Divinity, acknowledge that Catholics call that period of Jesus' life either the "Missing Years" or the "Hidden Years," and that mainstream Christianity cannot offer any information about those years except to speculate that Jesus was growing up in Judea with Joseph and Mary.

In the motion picture business, which has been my profession for three decades, we call the problem of the Missing Years a "jump cut." In the Bible, one moment young Jesus is twelve years old and speaking with the Jewish doctors of the law in the temple in Jerusalem. And then suddenly, on the next page, he's thirty years old being baptized at the River Jordan by his cousin, John the Baptist. Only one sentence in the **Gospel of Luke** (2:52) connects the years, and it says: "And Jesus increased in wisdom and stature and in favor with God and man." End of story.

But for Edward T. Martin, it was not the end of the story; it was the beginning of his own personal quest that has preoccupied him for most of his life, and which has now absorbed me for several years while making the film **"Jesus in India."**

We found some remarkable information, in some very amazing places. And there are reasons to take what these sources tell us quite seriously. But let's go further than the issue of the so-called "Missing

Years" or "Hidden Years." The very provocative question Christianity has avoided discussing since its inception is this: Is it possible that Jesus physically survived the crucifixion?

Until recent years, to even ask the question was considered blasphemy or heresy, and so parts of this investigation may still seem heretical to some. Christianity takes the Biblical accounts literally and states unequivocally that Jesus did die – and then He was resurrected and met with the Apostles, instructing them to preach the Gospel throughout the world. Then after a period of days, the "official story" asserts that he ascended to heaven to sit at the right hand of God, and that Jesus will return again – the Second Coming – to bring judgment upon all mankind in the Final Days.

Edward T. Martin no longer believes the "official story," but he believes there are many elements of historical fact in the New Testament concerning Jesus. In fact, he has tentatively concluded that the "official story" may have been a sort of "cover story," not unlike cover stories which may have been used to hide the fact that John Wilkes Booth probably did not really die after assassinating Lincoln, although it was made to appear that Booth did. Reports that Booth escaped and traveled to London by a ship departing San Francisco (the last possible place he would be expected to board to get to England), and that he even appeared on the stage again in London, are either nonsense or fact. People are free to reach either conclusion. But for those who look, there are clues to be followed, and there is testimony and evidence.

Medical science has advanced a long way in two thousand years, and today we know that the line between life and death is sometimes impossible to define. There have been many cases, in two thousand years, of people thought to be dead and nearly consigned to their graves, who were not dead at all and survived to tell their tales of "near death experiences."

Author Edward T. Martin takes as fact that Jesus did appear before his Apostles following the crucifixion. But he asks whether Jesus' actual survival could be a logical explanation for those sightings of Him, an explanation that does not depend upon the supernatural. Although he accepts that even Jesus' survival, under those circumstances, should be regarded as a great miracle, justifying the celebration of Easter, Ed searches for evidence that Jesus escaped the Roman Empire and had a continuing life in the east.

In the film, I sought many opinions other than those of Edward T. Martin. Five prominent Catholics weigh in on those questions, as well as a fundamentalist Christian preacher, Hindu priests, the Shankaracharya of the Hindu religion (one of the four ultimate ecclesiastical authorities on Hinduism, whose authority in the Hindu world is similar to that of the Pope in Catholicism), Buddhist monks in the Himalayas, a young Muslim scholar in London, a Jewish rabbi and many others. The Catholics appearing in the film include the late Monsignor Corrado Balducci, who was Apostolic Nuncio of John Paul II, Professors Alan C. Mitchell and Anthony Tambasco of Georgetown University, Michael Hesemann, who is a Vatican-accredited journalist, and Father Baptiste, who is the Catholic Bishop of Bareilly in India. Bestselling author Professor Elaine Pagels of Princeton University, who wrote **Beyond Belief: The Gospel of Thomas** and many other books, also made an important contribution to this film, conceding that: "We cannot rule out that Jesus may have traveled to India."

The Christian faithful (who pick up this book or who want to watch the DVD of the documentary feature motion picture, **"Jesus in India"**) need not fear that it is a one-sided diatribe, because it certainly is not. In fact, our assistant director on the film, Mr. N. T. Binny of Mumbai (whom everyone calls just "Binny"), is a devout "Thomas Christian" who said his prayers very early every morning while working on the film and who frequently reminded us that, although he could accept the evidence that Jesus possibly did journey to India as a young man, he believes the speculation about the crucifixion and its aftermath is unfounded. Jesus was resurrected and ascended to heaven, according to Binny. Nevertheless, Binny's curiosity was certainly piqued by the trail of inquiry, and he devoted every possible effort to helping us complete each phase of the production. He does not agree with some of Edward T. Martin's conclusions, but he believes it has taken a courage to pull back the veil and look at these issues.

Without resolving the questions raised in this book and in the film, which may never be resolved, we found that the trail of inquiry took us to Srinagar, to a specific grave believed by Ahmadiyya Muslims to be the final resting place of the historical Jesus Christ. We went there aware that political conflict and violence in the area made the visit dangerous – and made filming at the tomb in a Muslim district where the locals were angry at any intrusions and did not welcome visitors – even more dangerous.

The project meant so much to each of us involved in the filming of **"Jesus in India"** that we went there, in spite of the U.S. Secretary of State's admonitions for Americans considering such travel, and in spite of warnings at the tomb not to film it or photograph it even from the outside. That warning at the tomb appears as the final photograph of chapter twelve of this book.

Even stalwart believers in Jesus' resurrection may ask themselves what is so threatening, and to whom, that visitors would be warned not even to take a picture of a certain very ancient grave in northern India! And why does the grave have stone carvings of the feet of the prophet who is buried there, which suggest the wounds and scars of crucifixion? And why do some Christians as well as Ahmadiyya Muslims worship there, pay homage, light candles, shed tears – and why do all the other branches of Islam revere the tomb, protect it and discourage outsiders from approaching? There are three prophets in Islam – Abraham, Jesus and Mohammed – and the tomb in question is called by Muslims "The Prophet's Tomb." Neither Abraham nor Mohammed is buried there, so who is?

We survived the visit to Srinagar with extraordinary footage for our film. But others in that region, within the very next week, were not so lucky, and sixteen died. Terrorism continues there unabated, and most of it does not reach the western press. As this book is published, Kashmir has descended into bedlam, and many of those who live there are threatened.

My work on the film project did not end when the journey to India with Edward T. Martin was completed. There was still much to do and other travels to make. The filming continued at the Vatican, at Princeton University, Georgetown University, Amherst in Masssachusetts, Lampasas in Texas, London (home of Arif Khan), Florida (home of Suzanne Olsson), and many other places. I am indebted to many people for their contributions to this film. As for my time spent with Professor Elaine Pagels, interviewing her for the film brought me back to Princeton University, my alma mater, several decades after I had graduated as a young psychology student who had a particularly keen interest in making motion pictures.

The result of all of this is that I completed a motion picture about Edward T. Martin's search, **"Jesus in India."**

The search itself, as described by Edward T. Martin in this book, contains elements of both heaven and hell, and in many ways it enlightened us. Yes, we had some ecstatic experiences, seeing and beholding certain things and places holy to Hindus, Christians and Buddhists that are seldom seen by western eyes. Of our travels to about forty locations in India, there is little about it that was easy but there were parts of it that could be said to have been blessed.

I had many reasons for making **"Jesus in India,"** and the origins came about while I was a student at Princeton University. As an undergraduate student at the close of the 1960's, when it was still an all-male school, I took a course in Mahayama Buddhism, learned about the Maharishi Mahesh Yogi from the Beatles (and their dedication to the teacher known as Maharishi Mahesh Yogi and to Transcendental Meditation), and then I happened upon the "book of books" for mystical seekers, ***Autobiography of a Yogi***, by Paramahansa Yogananda.

I was raised as a non-practicing Jew by agnostic parents. However, my father was one of the few Jewish professors for forty years at Georgetown University, one of the most prominent Catholic institutions in the U.S. As a result of reading ***Autobiography of a Yogi***, while in college I attended services of Yogananda's Self-Realization Fellowship (SRF) in a private home about ten miles from Princeton.

I could scarcely have imagined at that time that I would end up studying film in Beverly Hills, at the American Film Institute Center for Advanced Film Studies, or that I would end up living for thirty years in a home atop a hill about half a mile from the Mount Washington "Mother Center" of Yogananda's Self-Realization Fellowship in Los Angeles, CA.

Nor could I have imagined then that Yogananda's writings, so filled as they are with devout belief in many seemingly "supernatural" realities, including the resurrection of Christ, would continue to hold a fascination for me and involve me throughout my life, including his teachings of Kriya Yoga.

My fellow producer on this project, who I invited to join me on this adventure, likewise was raised with ambiguous and conflicting religious realities. Anil Kumar Urmil was raised in Goa, India, the son of a Hindu father and a Catholic mother, both from India. He knew much about the travels of St. Thomas in India and had long heard tales about the travels of Jesus there. In making this film, he wanted to know more about whether he should believe the legends he had always heard, whether they had foundation in fact, or whether those stories should be regarded as myths.

Sometimes the answers we seek in life are not given to us. We must become a seeker to find them. We may never find them. But without the effort, without daring to try, there is never any result. The results of our questioning and our search for answers are offered with literary flair and considerable insight here by Edward T. Martin.

You will find not just what he feels we learned about the "King of Wisdom," as some have described Jesus in regard to his purported travels in India, but you will see the humor, heartaches and foibles of the author, who in some respects is just a very ordinary fellow who likes nothing more at the end of the day than to take off his leather cowboy boots and enjoy a Kingfisher Beer.

As a matter of fact, everyone who sees our film has a good laugh when Ed confesses how he first reacted when he heard the evidence that Mother Mary is buried in Pakistan and the mortal remains of Jesus are in a tomb in Kashmir.

"When I heard that, I needed another beer," he confessed.

As controversial as some aspects may prove to be, we gained confidence that we must have done something right when noted critic Pete Hammond wrote that **"'Jesus in India'** is a fascinating and profound film, a deeply spiritual journey certain to make you think and question in ways you never have before."

Edward T. Martin has done a wonderful job of taking you along with us to India and beyond. And so we both invite you to join us for the pages that follow, hoping you will experience and that you will learn, as we did, some absolutely fascinating things about the life of Jesus of Nazareth you didn't know before. As the Gospel of St. John says, "There are also many other things that Jesus did, which if they were written one by one, I suppose that even the world itself could not contain the books that would be written."

The poster of the film "Jesus in India"

The Prophet's Tomb in the Khanyar district of Srinagar, Kashmir,
where the prophet Yuz Asaf was laid to rest about 2,000 years ago.
Who was Prophet Yuz Asaf (also spelled Youza Asouph)?
And why does this tomb represent such a profound mystery?

PREFACE

By Edward T. Martin

Relatively few people are fortunate to have a movie - either documentary or theatrical - based upon their life's work. To my amazement, that is what happened to me.

In March of 2003, while attending a conference in Nevada, I met a novice screenwriter from southern California who also happened to be a very accomplished money manager at an international financial brokerage. I had a vendor's table there, and I was selling my book, ***King of Travelers: Jesus' Lost Years in India.***

At that time I had already made two trips to India where I had extensively researched the evidence that young Jesus may have spent time in India. That would be during the so called "Missing Years" in Jesus' life, between the ages of twelve to thirty.

The screenwriter, Mr. Robert Rotstan, Jr. ("call me Bob," he insisted immediately) met with me several times during the week-long conference; he asked a lot of good questions. In particular, "Do you think if someone were to make a movie about Jesus in India – either a documentary or theatrical – could it be a success?"

He had given a lot of thought to the question of Jesus' Missing Years himself and had undertaken special studies of the ancient origins of Christianity. Over the years, he had compiled a long list of questions about how Christianity grew to the shape and form it has today.

I told him, somewhat modestly, "Yes, I believe that if such a movie is made well, then a great many people would be motivated to watch it."

About the middle of the week, as the conference continued, Bob returned to my table with a distinguished-looking gentleman who also had a lot of good questions of his own. One of those was the same question as above. He then smiled, held out his hand and said, "You don't know who I am, do you?"

"No," I replied back with a smile, "should I? Are you someone important?"

He then introduced himself as Paul Davids, executive producer of the movie **"Roswell"** made in 1994 for the Showtime channel. That movie, starring Kyle MacLachlan, Dwight Yoakam and Martin Sheen, was about the 1947 Roswell, New Mexico UFO crash. Some of Paul's other movies include **"Timothy Leary's Dead"** (1997), **"Starry Night"** (2000) (a fantasy about Vincent Van Gogh), **"The Artist and the Shaman"** (2002) and **"The Sci-Fi Boys"** (2006). Paul bought a copy of my book and also a video tape of a talk/slide presentation I had given about Jesus in India in 2001.

ACROSS FROM THE CHINESE THEATRE

Paul and I talked several times later that week at the conference. He also gave me his business card and asked me to call him if I were to visit southern California.

In June of 2003, I was visiting friends in California and gave Paul a call. He, Bob Rotstan and I got together for lunch at Hamburger Hamlet, which was just across Hollywood Boulevard from Grauman's Chinese Theatre. (That icon of Hollywood has since been closed down, much to the disappointment of the natives who faithfully had "power lunches" at that Hamburger Hamlet for decades!)

We had a good discussion and then went to a movie premiere at Universal Studios. Paul had discussed then the possibility of getting financial backing to make a theatrical movie about Jesus in India. That didn't work out at that time, and I had to return to my activities in Texas.

We had also discussed the possibility of making a documentary movie if I were to return sometime to India. Things ended for the time on a somewhat unresolved note. Paul had a lot on his plate, professionally and personally. He seemed to close the door, at least for the time being, and as he said "Goodbye" on the phone I suspected that our meeting may have been a fluke, in vain so far as my larger goal was concerned.

How wrong that hunch proved to be. However, I drove in my car back to Texas and returned to my job teaching English as a second language, feeling somewhat disappointed. My life in Texas went on.

In the autumn of 2004, I began to think seriously about returning to India for more research in the summer of 2005. I began talking with filmmakers in the area of Austin, Texas (where I then lived) about a filming project to be developed from my research about Jesus' lost years in India. It seemed that everyone either was interested but had no money, or they had money but no interest in the project. About that time, I had a reading with a gifted young psychic named David Wilcock. I described the situation, and he told me that "Angelic helpers are ready, willing, and able to help with a Jesus in India movie. But you must specifically pray, asking for their help --- and, you must need the help!" So as Edwene Gaines said once, "I gave God a serious talking-to."

AN IMPORTANT PHONE CALL

The very next morning, in March of 2005, I phoned Jillian Burgin, a close friend of mine whom Paul had met at one of those conferences we so often attend – conferences that consider the points of view usually not embraced by the so-called "conventional Establishment" such as UFO's and extraterrestrials. She said she had run into Paul Davids when he was giving a lecture about his film **"Roswell"** and the controversial Roswell Incident. She had mentioned to him that I would be going to India for more Jesus in India research in the summer. She remarked that Paul "lit up like a Christmas tree" and had a lot of questions. She said, "I think you should give Paul a phone call and discuss this."

I also called Bob Rotstan, and he too suggested I call Paul and give it another try. So I soon called Paul Davids and discovered that his interest in doing a project with me was suddenly "off the charts" it was so intense. I was frankly surprised at discovering how serious he was about pursuing it – it seemed like a dramatic turn-around for him. He promised me a firm answer in one or two days. He was no longer interested in a dramatic film about this subject using actors, but he was very much interested in accompanying me to India and making a documentary movie, based on my new research and loosely based upon my book about Jesus in India, ***King of Travelers: Jesus' Lost Years in India.***

Paul explained that he would like to bring on board his colleague, Anil Kumar Urmil, as part of our team to produce the film with him. Anil, who was then living in southern California, was originally from Goa in western India and had influential contacts throughout the country. Also, he had worked with Paul making **"Starry Night."**

Paul also explained that before such a project could begin, he and I would need to have a written and signed contract. That detail was taken care of quickly.

Most of the events described in this book took place in India during the summer of 2005. Paul later continued the work in Italy (at the Vatican and other locations), England and the United States in the autumn of 2005 and on into 2006.

Paul, Anil, and I were accompanied in India by our Indian staff: an assistant director, a production manager, a travel agent, associate producers, key contacts in each major city we had as a destination, and a second-unit cameraman (Paul did the principal photography). We traveled for six weeks on a journey of more than 4,000 miles throughout India.

We traveled in a great, counter-clockwise circle by train, bus, van, car, foot, boat, rickshaw, elephant, taxi, and sometimes airplanes. We visited monasteries, temples, ashrams, churches, libraries, and ancient archives. We conducted interviews with a wide range of authorities and researchers.

At the end of our amazing journey, we had a massive amount of footage. We had many brushes with danger, and the challenge (and frequent discomfort en route) was intensified by the fact that we undertook this during monsoon season and at the height of the summer heat.

But we survived!

And the results are something we are all proud of to this day.

We sincerely hope the results of our efforts may help others on their own unique spiritual journeys.

So welcome aboard – the India Express is about to depart the station!

Table of Contents

JESUS IN INDIA: KING OF WISDOM

THE MAKING OF THE FILM & NEW FINDINGS ON JESUS' LOST YEARS

"We are going again, this time to Central Asia, where, if anywhere upon earth, wisdom is to be found, and we anticipate that our journey will be a long one."

— H. Rider Haggard, **She**

Image of Jesus in the Basilica of St. Francis Xavier in Goa, India

1. Rendezvous in Goa

"A journey of a thousand miles begins with but a single step."
---Ancient Chinese Proverb

With a roar, the Aeroflot jet began the final descent to Indira Gandhi International Airport. This was my third journey to India, and I was thrilled to be back! On my two previous trips, I had researched the evidence that young Jesus had lived and studied in India. My first book, **King of Travelers: Jesus' Lost Years in India**, was based on that research. I was returning now to join a team of professional filmmakers who would make a documentary movie based on my research.

After the aircraft came to a complete stop, I unfastened my seatbelt and took a single step into a great new adventure. It was about 2:30 a.m. on a hot morning in early June of 2005. I would be meeting my contact, Rajneesh, there at the New Delhi airport.

This was the beginning of an amazing six-week long journey, ultimately traveling more than 4,000 miles throughout India. There would be six members on our filming team. Paul Davids, a professional filmmaker (producer / screenwriter / director) from southern California would be our leader, director, producer and first cameraman (director of photography).

Anil Kumar Urmil would serve as producer with Paul. His brother-in-law, H. R. Madhusudan (whom we all called "Madhu"), would serve as our production manager while we were in India. Nelvan Thomas Binny, affectionately called "Binny" by everyone, would be Paul's assistant director, and Dnyanesh Moghe ("DM") was our second cameraman and associate producer for India, along with Sanjay Shetye, who was also associate producer for India as well as our travel agent. Our whole team would rendezvous in Goa at Vasco da Gama City and begin our journey from there.

And what an adventure it would be!

Welcome to India in 2005

THE ADVENTURE BEGINS

Rajneesh Charan, Anil Urmil's tall cousin, who had a very serious demeanor and was the father of a baby girl who was born quite recently, met me with a hand-lettered sign bearing my name. I had already retrieved my two bags and had passed quickly through customs.

We stepped outside into some remarkably hot air for 2:45 in the morning! We were in a fog-like haze of what appeared to be floating dust particles and exhaust fumes.

Rajneesh took me in his small car to the apartment complex where he, his wife, and new-born daughter live. The complex appeared to be made of cinder blocks.

We climbed the stairs to the third floor (there was no elevator, something I would have to get used to in many multi-story buildings in India). Graciously, Rajneesh, along with his wife and daughter, had moved out of their main bedroom which was cooled by a "swamp cooler" or evaporative cooling device such as those commonly used in the southwest United States.

As their guest, I slept there while they stayed in the guest bedroom with a small electric fan. The swamp cooler did a reasonably effective job of reducing the sweltering temperature, and I was grateful for it. I fell asleep immediately.

THE CALLS OF A PEACOCK

I woke up in mid-morning to the raucous and exotic calls of a peacock in a field nearby. On my first two journeys to India I had heard peacocks before and now a lot of good memories came back. I rubbed my eyes, rolled over on the mattress and squinted, looking outside through a hole in the swamp cooler.

It was a bright , sunny, hot day. I could see acacia-type thorn trees in the rocky fields below. Also, I could hear the sounds of traffic in the vicinity, because we were not far from the New Delhi Airport. What adventures, I wondered, would lie ahead?

Rajneesh knocked on the door and told me cheerfully that breakfast was ready. His wife, wearing a traditional sari, greeted me warmly. Their baby daughter relaxed on a blanket on the floor, playing with her feet.

As I drank a cup of hot tea with milk and sugar, the telephone rang. It was our producer, Anil, calling from Goa, the old Portuguese colony south of Bombay. Anil and Paul Davids both spoke with me, explaining that their airplane journey from Los Angeles had gone well. They had arrived safely in Mumbai (Bombay) and then had proceeded to Goa. They were now in Vasco Da Gama City, at the home of Anil's

Rajneesh Charan, the first contact from our film to meet me in India

parents, where they had already been filming for a couple of days.

They had already gotten some good footage along the seacoast of fishermen, boats and the native population tending to rice paddies and the fields, as well as footage in a temple dedicated to Sai Baba (an Indian saint to both Hindus and Muslims), where the congregation allowed them to film a ceremony.

There was also their journey to film at the Church of the Three Kings, a small but spectacular stone church on the coast where a carefully tended fire burned through the night right outside, the flickering flames illuminating the front door.

They explained that Madhu had arranged for us to take up residence at a government guest cottage in Goa, and they gave me the information necessary to get my airplane ticket the next morning to join them.

After breakfast, Rajneesh and I went in his car to a cell phone shop to try to buy an activation chip for the new phone I had bought in Texas for our trip. There was a glitch. The new phone would not activate. Later, Paul and Anil told me not to worry, because we already had several cell phones in our group.

Two of my shirts, which were supposed to be ready with a speedy "next morning" service, were not ready then. The laundry, like so many laundries in India, didn't have clothes dryers. Clothes are dried in the sunlight under the sweltering summer heat, not by machine. However, when there's a storm, one waits for one's clothes for an extra day or more. Such was the case then, unfortunately. But I had an appointment for Goa and could not wait around an extra day or two for my shirts to dry. So I smiled and told the laundry people to save my clothes for me, because I would be back in five or six weeks. In the meantime, I could easily buy more shirts!

I thought to myself that the journey was just beginning, and it seemed that Mercury was already in retrograde!

I bought some sweetmeats (they are not actually meat; they are a sweet type of dessert morsels) covered with a traditional layer of very thin, edible silver. I presented the box of goodies to Rajneesh and his wife. After breakfast, he and I then went in his car to the airport. I thanked him and then took my luggage to the Indian Airlines counter. I smiled, pressed my palms together and gave a "namaste" greeting. I then gave the paper with the flight information and authorization code. Soon, I had my ticket and was on my way.

The flight had a brief stopover in Mumbai to transfer passengers. It was still difficult for me to think of the city as being named Mumbai rather than Bombay, which is the name by which Americans and the British have always known it. However, as with a number of other places in India, I had no choice but to quickly adjust myself to the return to the original, native place names. It's not unlike the situation in China, where after a lifetime of saying Peking we suddenly had to get used to Beijing. The same is true of the place names of many locations in Africa, which have been returned to their original, native names.

As we flew in to Mumbai, I could see a great number of makeshift shacks and hovels just outside the airport security fence. The poverty in that city, and in fact in many cities of India, is heartwrenching. However, a great mass of humanity is adjusted to living in shacks with almost no material goods, because they have absolutely no choice. Many of the shacks of Mumbai do have electricity, but it is sometimes a danger to the residents. Wiring is often low-lying, close to the ground, and when it floods, people can easily be electrocuted. (This actually happened on the day of Paul and Anil's departure nearly two months later, when a storm dumped thirty-three inches of rain on Mumbai in a single-day and nearly one thousand people died, most by electrocution! However, I get far ahead of myself, because this journey was just beginning…)

Beyond the shacks of Mumbai, there are the more affluent buildings and skyscrapers of the great metropolis. The contrast is unbelievable, because it is like two entirely different worlds existing side by side. It is always poignant to see the disparities of life. However, soon we were airborne again and those thoughts faded from my mind. And before long, I was about to embark on a rendezvous at Goa.

As the Indian Airlines jet descended toward Goa in a clear, sunny sky, I thought about the goals of this trip. In my first book, **King of Travelers: Jesus' Lost Years in India**, I had written in detail about how I first got on the trail of the myths, legends and actual evidence that Jesus spent part of his life in India.

My questioning about the unaccounted for years of Jesus began while I was still in grade school in Texas, going to Bible school every week to learn about the Lord. Bible school teachers couldn't answer my questions about those Missing Years, so I took solace in the writings and teachings of people such as Edgar Cayce and Levi Dowling.

Was it possible that Jesus had really journeyed to India? The whole idea gained credibility for me, and all the more so when I encountered the claims about this by Indian philosopher Paramahansa Yogananda.

Soon I was reading Nicolas Notovitch's **The Unknown Life of Jesus Christ**, which the Russian explorer claimed was a translation of an ancient Tibetan document that filled in the Missing Years of Jesus in great detail.

I wanted to verify that the ancient manuscript Notovitch had seen and described actually existed. It was one of my unfulfilled goals in life. And so of course I hoped our filming team would make the journey to Hemis Monastery at the top of the world, so to speak, at 14,000 foot elevation in the Himalayas, where Notovitch said he first encountered that manuscript and that material.

A bronze bust of Paramahansa Yogananda presented in honor
of the centennial of his birth, in Kolkata (Calcutta)

However, there were other ways to verify the existence of the manuscript short of actually finding it. That part of the research would take us to Calcutta, now known as Kolkata. Not only was that the home city of Paramahansa Yogananda and Mother Teresa, it was also home to the late Swami Abhedananda. The great Swami, a direct disciple of Ramakrishna and Vivekananda, had lived for twenty-five years in America, during which time he encountered Notovitch's controversial book. Swami Abhedananda had returned to India, to Kolkata, and from there had staged a journey to the Hemis Monastery. In his writings, including ***Journey to Kashmir and Tibet***, he tells how he verified Notovitch's claims. I felt that if our filming team were to go to Kolkata and visit the Ramakrishna Vedanta Math, where Swami Abhedananda had lived, we could learn more about this process of verification from his disciples.

It was also long rumored that Swami Abhendananda had received a very ancient drawing of Jesus from Notovitch, which he kept at his home in Kolkata, and if it was still there, I wanted to see it and film it. There were so many other goals to our journey, it all flooded my mind during that plane flight, and especially during our slow descent toward Goa. In Hinduism, reportedly for over two thousand five hundred years, there has been a position known as the Shankaracharya. As I indicated earlier, it's somewhat akin to being the Pope in Catholicism, because at any given time, the Shankaracharya has eccliastical authority over millions of Hindus. A previous Shankaracharya had provided information about Jesus in India to one of Yogananda's successors as

A statue of a Christian Saint in the Basilica of
St. Francis of Xavier, in Goa, India

head of the Self-Realization Fellowship in Los Angeles, Sri Daya Mata. She has told of hearing direct verification that the very ancient Hindu temple in Puri, known as the Jagannath Temple on the northeast coast of India, has ancient records that confirm young Jesus was there and in fact studied there. This parallels precisely information that is in the book by Levi Dowling, ***The Aquarian Gospel,*** and also Notovitch's ***The Secret Life of Jesus Christ.***

Could the current Shankaracharya be persuaded to discuss this matter? And would he agree to be interviewed on camera? We had been told that the Shankaracharya <u>never</u> gives public interviews, and certainly not filmed interviews. Nevertheless, we wished to accomplish the impossible.

And there was so much more to answer. Did the Dalai Lama know of Jesus in India? Could we gain audience with him at his headquarters in Dharamshala in the Himalayan foothills?

What was known about this topic at the International Society for Krishna Consciousness Temple (ISKCON) in Bangalore? Reportedly they had ancient records that had been transcribed into a computer databank, and the leader of this Hindu group, Swami Prabhupada, had reportedly made reference to this information on several occasions.

There were also Indian Catholic priests to interview and the head priests of the Hindu Meenakshi Temple of Madurai. Would they speak with us? What would we learn? And what about the Buddhists of isolated regions such as Sikkim. What could they tell us?

My heart beat swiftly as I excitedly thought about all of these great and challenging goals of our filming journey. The only thing that could distract me from such thoughts was the colossal view beneath me.

I looked below in fascination. So far, I had traveled on six continents in fifty-seven countries. Still, I am keenly interested whenever I arrive in a place that is new for me, that I have not seen before. I had heard stories for years about the former Portuguese colony of Goa in western India. I was impressed now by the beautiful reddish-orange color of the earth below and the exotic, cactus-type plants. The Indian Ocean stretched to the west. I thought of the same type of soil in East Africa and how that many millions of years ago, it is believed that India, Madagascar and East Africa had all been adjoined together in a great land mass. And, of course, with continental drift, India had moved northward eventually colliding with Asia, creating the Himalayas in the process.

As the plane landed, I gathered my thoughts and looked at my contact paper. Madhu would be meeting me with a paper sign outside of the baggage claim area. An officer in the Indian Navy, Madhu greeted me cheerfully and helped me with my baggage. He then drove me to the Government Guest House which overlooks the ocean from a hillside at Mormugao.

H. R. Madhusudan ("Madhu"), Anil's brother-in-law,
coordinated many details of our production in India

Two porters carried my luggage, and I was soon in a comfortable, air-conditioned room. Madhu left to take care of other arrangements.

We would all have a get-together that evening at the home of Anil's parents. I was told that Paul Davids and the rest of the crew were out filming at that moment, and I would rendezvous with them later. A servant arrived with a steaming pot of tea and some cookies.

I soon went for a walk outside in the beautiful gardens. The weather was hot and very humid. I was thankful that for much of our future journey we would be in air-conditioned places!

Wild mynah birds perched overhead on some tree branches as I strolled around. To my surprise, I saw a wild lemur nearby under some bushes. Lemurs are somewhat similar to raccoons, but they have long, banded tails and more slender bodies. I knew that lemurs are native to

Madagascar but had not expected to see them in western India. The next day, at the house of Anil's parents, we saw several lemurs playing in the trees and on the ground nearby.

A HILLTOP VIEW OF THE OCEAN

The room at the guest house was rather Spartan, with no television, radio or pictures on the walls. I had a small battery-powered shortwave radio, my Bell & Howell, and was able to pick up a BBC newscast. Why was it that so much of the news had to concern acts of terrorist violence?

The government guest house in Goa where our film crew stayed

In England, fears were intensifying of a possible attack on civilians, because there had been many threats. And in India, where I had arrived after such a long journey, the conflicts between Hindus and Muslims continued.

Many communities of different religions did live in harmony in India. But there were extremists with their own agendas on both sides, which had been the case ever since India and Pakistan were established as two separate nations in 1947. Conflict and dispute over the province known as "Jammu and Kashmir" was heating up. Every day civilians died from violent acts in the very part of the nation we would be visiting.

I turned the air conditioning to the low setting and laid down for a nap. Madhu returned about sunset in the SUV. We drove to the home of Anil's parents for dinner and a welcoming party. I was delighted to see my friend, Paul Davids, again and also happy to meet Anil Urmil, whom Paul had invited to produce the film with him. Anil's parents greeted me warmly, and I was soon handed a glass of cold Indian beer. After all the hot weather, the beer was welcome!

I learned later to practice moderation because the alcohol content of Indian beer is significantly higher than American beer!

Anil's mother and father hosted our arrival
on his mother's birthday

Anil's father is a physician and a retired military officer and has a treasure trove of personal stories from an adventure-filled lifetime.

Paul soon had his camera set up on the tripod and was interviewing Anil's father in the adjoining bedroom. *India Today*, a magazine reminiscent of *Time* or *Newsweek* in the United States, had just published an article citing the widespread belief among people in Kashmir that Jesus had been to their homeland. Anil's father was busy explaining the significance of the article.

Dinner was very tasty, and after much conversation with the guests I was feeling sleepy. I was still recovering from some jet lag!

After dinner, Madhu took Paul and me back to the guest house. With the air conditioning on a low setting I was soon asleep.

I woke up around daybreak to the sound of rain drops hitting the roof. I stood up and moved the curtains to peer through the window. The sky was gray and overcast with a drizzling rain falling. It was the second week in June. The monsoon rains would begin soon.

The monsoon normally begins in the far south of India and moves northward, so our plan was to quickly travel to our southern-most point, Madurai. From there we would travel northward, hope-fully keeping ahead of the rains coming behind us. However, what if our plans were to go awry and we were to have continous rain every day for six weeks? So I did what I've been doing all my life to try to ward off misfortune. I prayed.

FIRST RENDEZVOUS AT GOA

After breakfast, the rain stopped and the sun came out. Paul and I descended the flight of stairs (no elevator in the government guest house, either) and loaded our bags into an air-conditioned SUV. The driver took us to Anil's place. There, we had a rendezvous with our whole six-member filming team: Paul, Anil, myself, Binny, Madhu and Dnyanesh Moghe.

We had a train to catch and we were all hustling to get our lug-gage and equipment ready. Anil told us that we should all minimize our personal effects to one medium or small-sized piece of baggage per person. Besides that, we had two fairly large cases for our video cameras, two large tripods in cases, and assorted other filming equip-ment and paraphernalia. In all, we set out with 14 pieces of luggage! We also had plastic bottles of clean drinking water, personal cameras, caps, hats, sunglasses and so forth.

Anil's parents graciously allowed us to store any surplus luggage at their home, knowing that at the conclusion of the production in India, Anil and Paul would be coming back to their home.

We kept looking at our watches as we carried baggage outside into two SUVs with drivers who were waiting for us. About that time,

Dealing with luggage for the India travels was always a challenge

I heard singing from the living room. It was Anil's mother's birthday, and candles were burning on a cake. A little, impromptu party was going on!

Despite the pressing rush (we had scarcely fifteen minutes before our train was scheduled to leave the station), Paul and I quickly stuffed down a piece of cake, and we sang "Happy Birthday" with mouths full of crumbs.

We were nearing a state of panic, but Madhu remained calm, telling us not to worry because the train station was only five minutes away – we had plenty of time! But luggage was not all loaded into the vehicle yet, and some of it had to be strapped on top! No worry, said Madhu. That would take less than five minutes. There would still be two to five minutes to spare!

As fate would have it, it was fortunate we devoted that time, even those few minutes, to that very rushed birthday celebration. It was the last birthday for Anil's mother, who had been experiencing heart ailments for many months. She died not long after our return to the United States, a very sad moment.

With icing and cake crumbs smeared across our faces, each member of our team was dabbing his face with napkins, as we scooted out the door and hurried down several flights of stairs.

We were very quickly on our way to the Vasco Da Gama train station. Our driver said something to me in Hindi which I understood and answered.

Paul seemed surprised, "You speak Hindi?"

"Just some basic things, simple things," I said. I had a Hindi language tutor when I was in the Peace Corps in Afghanistan.

"That may come in handy," Paul replied.

Outside the train station we assembled our baggage into a big pile with maddening haste. I was impressed by how much equipment we still had, even after "paring things down."

Some pieces of baggage looked huge ---and heavy! Anil had us remove any paper remnants of airline tags from our luggage, so we wouldn't look like wealthy tourists who could afford airline tickets!

AT THE VASCO DA GAMA TRAIN STATION

Quickly, there were five or six stalwart porters who approached us from the station. Anil and our other Indian staff did some rapid-fire Hindi language negotiations and our whole entourage was soon moving at the most brisk pace imaginable. We could hear our train approaching the station, as the bags were just being removed from our van.

Standing on the platform near our train was Sanjay Shetye, one of our two associate producers for India, who was also our travel agent. He was with another young man, Govind, his assistant.

Sanjay was a maestro at making travel arrangements, which he usually did from his small and very crowded office, just alongside a restaurant that he owned and which did a booming business.

From Sanjay, I was reminded of one rather amusing difference in customs between the people of India and Americans. We shake our heads left and right, back and forth, to mean <u>no</u>. When someone from India shakes his head from that way, it means <u>yes</u>! And usually the head bobs a bit at the same time, a most peculiar gesture from our point of view, but that is quite the norm in India.

When I pressed Sanjay, asking him if he thought all our luggage would be on the train station boarding platform by the time the train came to a stop, he shook his head swiftly from left to right and I thought he was saying "<u>no way</u>!" But he meant quite the opposite.

*Sanjay Shetye (left) and Paul Davids have a beer during
a production meeting before departing for Bangalore*

All of our train tickets and hotel arrangements and so forth were worked out in advance, thanks to Sanjay and his capable staff.

Whenever we had any question or problem we could always reach Sanjay on one of our cell phones. He always worked out a solution, and several times, such as when we were trapped in Kashmir with no way to depart, he worked miracles. Joking and laughing, we were all in high spirits and eager to begin our great adventure as the porters loaded our bags into the train!

The train whistle soon blew and we had only seconds left to board. We said thanks and farewell to Sanjay and his helper; we would see them later in our journey. Binny showed Paul and me to our sleeper berths which served as seats for the time being, at least until well after nightfall.

Paul and Binny had a splendid rapport, but then again, Binny's wonderful good nature helped him to get along with everyone. Binny treated all people with great respect. It was his way, and part of his religious belief. Paul had agreed to hire Binny as assistant director without even having met him, on Anil's recommendation. Anil simply assured Paul that he had the best man for the job, and that Binny could be relied upon for handling everything, twenty-four seven, as we say. And that was true.

After the train pulled out of the station, we soon began to see beautiful white sand beaches on the right side. There were also a lot of coconut palms, and the ocean waves were spectacular. Paul and Anil talked about how they might even buy some real estate in the area, but it was one of those conversations that sounded more like an idle dream than serious talk. I did gather, however, that real estate values in Goa often are superb. For a fraction of what it would cost to buy beach property in the U.S., one could have quite a nice little estate in Goa.

Paul joked with DM about that, saying that he could get to the beach in forty-five minutes from where he lived in Los Angeles. He didn't have to take a twenty-four hour plane flight to get to Goa so the beach could be right outside his door.

DM proceeded to try to convince Paul that it would be worth it to fly that twenty-four hours to swim at the beaches of Goa, far superior to the beach at Santa Monica, and besides, wouldn't Paul love to set up a post-production facility in Goa while he was at it? It would be just a short trip by plane to Bollywood in Mumbai!

I found DM to be humorous and good-natured, always able to turn a serious conversation to comedy to lighten everyone's mood. Every team going on an adventure needs a comedian, I thought, and we had one. A comedian plus an incurable sleight-of-hand magician (Paul).

The train soon took us on a more inland route. We were headed southeastward on an overnight journey to Bangalore, and we intended to visit the International Society for Krishna Consciousness headquarters, or ISKCON. It was situated in an unbelievably majestic white temple, with interior displays of great jewels adorning the statues of Krishna and Radha, his beloved. Those sights in the temple were usually hidden from the eyes of westerners, but we hoped that we might be granted the chance to see them. Our hopes were not to be dashed.

The headquarters of the International Society for
Krishna Consciousness (ISKCON), located in Bangalore

After the ISKCON visit we would be heading for Madurai, in far
south India, site of the astonishing Meenakshi Temple.

The Meenakshi Temple has many tower structures resembling
pyramids rising up from the central complex. The towers are very
high, very ancient and covered with colorful statues – thousands of
them – of all the deities of Hindu mythology.

The train went into mountains and we were passing through jungles all around. Binny and Madhu came to tell us that in half an hour
or so we would pass by a spectacular waterfall, truly a waterfall so
beautiful it could be considered one of the wonders of the natural
world. It was essential that Paul film it, but it would be a matter of

split second timing. He would have a warning of less than thirty seconds to prepare.

Concern that he might miss getting the waterfall weighed like a shadow on Paul's face. He had been filming scenery through the open windows of the train, but to film the waterfall properly, he would have to be set up in the open passageway between two train cars.

A WONDROUS WATERFALL

As the train continued its forward motion, swaying and shifting, Binny held a tight grip with one of his hands at the back of Paul's belt, literally to keep Paul from plunging off the train. Binny's other hand gripped tightly to a metal railing on the train. Paul adjusted the camera and leaned alertly to the right, where the waterfall would appear.

Soon, through the trees and tropical vegetation, we could see the breathtaking waterfall ahead. I had traveled the world and seen many waterfalls, but this was truly, without exaggeration, one of the most beautiful cascades in existence, coming from the heights above, and spreading across a broad, rocky part of the mountainside.

Paul did his best to remain calm but focused and efficient, with barely twenty seconds to get the shot, and only one chance to get it.

Having accomplished the filming with hardly a second to spare, Paul grinned at us, made a thumbs up, and Binny pulled him back to safety.

The train trip from Goa to Bangalore was truly scenic in the greatest sense of the word. We watched a lovely sunset and then Madhu appeared with steaming cardboard boxes of chicken biryani (a chicken and rice meal) with fresh, hot naan (an Indian flatbread). A train employee brought us traditional Indian tea with milk and sugar.

After dinner, Paul performed one of his impromptu magic shows, to the delight of the nearby passengers, including several children. However, the delight was mixed with dismay, because it was impossible to figure out how he accomplished any of his skillful feats, as much as one wanted to catch him at his trickery. He used a deck of cards, some coins, a small square of silk, finger rings and other simple objects. He baffled everyone, including me!

(A year or so later, Paul took me, along with Brian Lambert, composer of the musical score for **"Jesus in India,"** to the Magic Castle in Hollywood, California, where we saw some really amazing magic. Paul has been a member at the Magic Castle since 1986, back in the days when he was the production coordinator of the daily **"Trans-formers"** cartoon show.)

The train continued its steady progress through the night. Some people played cards, laughed and smoked cigarettes. I walked forward to a place between cars, held a railing carefully and peered up thoughtfully at the starry night. Binny, Madhu and I would sometimes joke and say, "It's Paul's favorite kind of night: a starry night!" (That's because of his movie about Vincent van Gogh, **"Starry Night,"** which was named after one of van Gogh's most famous paintings, and also the lines in Don McLean's song, **"Vincent,"** which became the theme song of that film.)

When I was finally ready to fade off to sleep, I unfolded the clean cotton sheets and wool blanket which the train provides and comfortably stretched out on the cushioned bunk.

Life can be strange, I thought. I know it's a cliché to say it, but I really did pinch myself to make sure that everything happening was not just a dream. But it was all for real! I was actually back in India, and this time a professional filming team was with me! And we were making a movie based on my book and continuing research! Wow!

I thought about how I had been ostracized from my church, after having been a devoted and loyal member of the congregation since I was old enough to sit in a pew and listen to a sermon. I was reminded of the painful feelings of becoming essentially "persona non grata" in my own hometown, because I had the audacity to ask penetrating questions about the religion I had been taught, and because I had "strayed" by "thinking outside the box." In my case, the "box" was the New Testament of the Bible. My friends and neighbors believed every word of it was true, that it was the infallible, inspired word of God. However, how much did they even know about its contradictions and missing pieces? Why weren't any of them even curious about the "hole in history" in the New Testament, the failure to mention anything specific about Jesus' life from the time he was twelve up until his thirtieth year? For them, I was the square peg in the round hole, the oddball, the one who couldn't just fit in, the "troublemaker." I had the unacceptable gall to ask the wrong question and want the answer too badly, and so I no longer fit in, and they did not miss me.

With the gentle rocking movement of the train, I was soon able to put those negative thoughts of the past out of my mind. I turned my thoughts to the excitement ahead, and I drifted into a deep sleep.

2. Night Train to Bangalore and ISKCON

"It is better to aim at a lion and miss,
than to aim at a jackal and kill it."
---folk saying from India

I woke up in the darkness in my bunk, amidst the rocking and swaying of the motion of the train. For a few puzzled seconds, I could not figure out where I was or what was happening. "Oh yes," I told myself, "I'm back in India on a train." I sat upright in my clothes, realizing that I was wide awake and not about to return to sleeping very quickly. Quietly, while those in the other bunks slept, I put on my boots and walked carefully down the corridor to the restroom.

After using the restroom, standing between two cars of the swaying train, I stared up at the vast number of bright stars, including the broad swath of the Milky Way, seen on its side. "The backbone of the night," as the bushmen of South Africa call it.

My mind was filled with thoughts of a journey of my younger days, when I was in the Peace Corps in Afghanistan in 1974. I was in a bar having a beer, and the label said Murree Beer. I recalled the conversation I had with the bartender about that strange name on the bottle of beer. It was named after a town in Pakistan, said the bartender, a town where Mary, Mother of Jesus, was buried. Murree, he said, was a mis-spelling of her name that stuck through the centuries. Even then, while standing between two cars on the rumbling, racing train, I could easily re-experience my shock and amazement at even hearing such a preposterous thing.

I had been raised in the Church of Christ. We certainly did not believe that Mary, Mother of Jesus, was buried in Pakistan. Catholics believe that she ascended bodily to heaven, and that is the explanation for why her grave in Jerusalem is empty. The Church of Christ never occupied itself with such things, but Pakistan was too far from the Holy Land for the idea even to have been a possibility. The bartender had explained to me that Jesus had not died on the cross, that he had survived the crucifixion and was helped to escape from his tomb. As a survivor, Jesus had appeared secretly to his disciples, who concluded that he had been resurrected from the dead. So to avoid being put to death "again," he fled from Judea with his mother, first going to Damascus in Syria, where he was seen by the Saul of Tarsus who later became the Apostle Paul after seeing and hearing what he thought was the "resurrected" Jesus. Then, according to the Pakistani bartender, Jesus continued on toward Kashmir, site of one of the Lost Tribes of Israel, and his mother Mary died along the way. Thus her tomb is in Pakistan.

For years I experienced a swirl of chaotic and confused thoughts about all of that, but now, with what I had learned since that fateful day, I took it all much more in stride, and for reasons that you will discover the story has become very real for me.

Soon I was lifted from my thoughts by the arrival of daybreak. I returned to my bunk. Others were still sleeping, but not for long. A young vendor on the train was calling out: "Chai! Chai garam!" (Tea! Hot tea!)

I smiled and motioned him over, handing him a coin.

I sat up and nestled the warm paper cup in my two hands. A beautiful clear day was dawning; we would soon be approaching Bangalore.

The tea vendors always woke up the sleeping passengers on Indian trains very early in the morning. One's chances of sleeping much beyond six a.m. were practically nil.

Of course, in our film crew, there would always be one of us who would never be allowed to sleep at all. With all of our valuable filming equipment with us, we could not risk the possibility of theft, which sometimes happens to sleeping travelers who are not cautious. One among us, every night, was assigned to remain awake to "guard" our equipment. After difficult, hot days of work, it was a terrible challenge and almost impossible to keep from nodding off. But we each took our turn at some point during the journey, and when it was our turn, we had to try to ward off sleep.

After the train stopped that glorious morning, we assembled our baggage on the platform and began our "snake" to the train hotel rooms at the far end of the platform. The "snake" was what I called our common sense method for six adults to move fourteen pieces of baggage safely from one location to another within walking distance – at the times when we had no porters. We would first make restroom trips as needed while several of us stayed with the "baggage mountain." Then one of us – often Anil – would take a seat and be the "anchor" while the rest of us began carrying or rolling luggage.

It is no secret that the journey was even more of a challenge for Anil than for the rest of us. Anil, who was producing the film with

Paul, had polio in childhood. He could walk fine with the help of a leg brace and cane, but on a trip like this one, in addition to the fourteen pieces of luggage, we had Anil's wheel-chair.

It was a testament to his courage, determination and bravery that he never let his impediment get in his way or stop him from reaching any destination. Whether using a cane or seated in a wheelchair, Anil was with us from the hot and humid jungles of the southlands of India to the cool breezes of the Himalayan mountains.

Porters in India carry luggage on their heads,
even if the luggage has wheels!

He was there, whether with cane or seated in his wheel-chair, in the great ancient Hindu Temples, the Buddhist monasteries and even at Saint Thomas Mount in Chennai, where the Apostle Thomas lived and preached in India in the years following the crucifixion.

Anyway, regarding our "snake" to transport luggage, at our destination we would have another person sit as "anchor" to guard the ever-growing baggage pile. After several relay trips we would have everything moved to the new location. Without a system like this, luggage left unguarded would probably simply disappear quickly. Whenever widespread poverty and physical hardship exists, as is found in so

Producer Anil Urmil (right) with assistant director
"Binny" (Nelvan Thomas Binny)

many places in India, there are among the majority of honest and religious people a certain number of agile and alert thieves. Those who are neither cautious nor mindful of their own protection are simply asking for trouble.

We had two private rooms at the train station reserved for the day. We would be leaving around sunset on an overnight train to our next destination, Madurai, in far south India.

We could safely lock our luggage up for the day while we rented an air-conditioned SUV and a driver to take us to that day's filming locations. Although the train station rooms were spartan, they had restrooms and showers, simple beds and air conditioning (which worked at least somewhat). Metal bars on the windows and heavy padlocks on the doors completed the security.

TO THE ISKCON TEMPLE

After we "freshened up," as Anil would say, we shouldered our camera gear and trooped out to the front of the railway station. Our two camera tripods (still about three feet long, even when telescoped in completely) seemed always to be a magnet for a flurry of attention.

The tripods seemed to tip everyone off that some kind of "professional" filming activity was underway. And therefore, some company with deep pockets might be willing to pay extra for rental of the best vehicles with extra-good air conditioning, the best guides, and so on.

At times like that, Paul and I kept an extra-low profile and let Anil and our other staff do all of the high-spirited bargaining in whatever language was appropriate. One thing that was certainly true about India – bargaining was usually high-spirited, fast-paced, soft then loud then rising to a shout, tit for tat, thrust for parry. Whether the amount being debated was ten dollars or five hundred, the drama was usually the same. At one point in our journey, I recall a robust negotiation that went on for nearly fifteen minutes about a ten dollar tip that a boatman expected to be paid. You would have thought it was the President and his cabinet arguing about a billion dollar budget item!

We were soon squared away and careened off on our way to the magnificent ISKCON Temple of Bangalore. The temple was built by and is maintained by the International Society for Krishna Consciousness, sometimes referred to in America as the Hare Krishna Society. We drove up to the impressive, large white temple which is located on a hilltop within Bangalore city. Thankfully, we were able to park under a covered parking area, which gave blissful shade from the very hot sun.

In that I was recovering from an upset stomach, I was happy to let Paul, Anil and our other staff do the scheduled interview with the Hindu priest at the temple. They met with a young priest who was most knowledgeable regarding the temple's computer data-base. The founder of ISKCON, A. C. Bhaktivedanta Swami Prabhupada, was reported to have had some knowledge about Jesus in India which it turned out the priests were in fact able to summon up for us on the ISKCON computers. Talk about a marriage between ancient lore and modern technology! Every word uttered by Swami Prabhupada or written in his copious writings apparently was available at the click of a mouse on a computer screen in that very well-endowed temple. Jesus in India was a subject that Swami Prabhupada had weighed in on, and amazingly, he had once gotten into a conversation on the subject with American beat poet Allen Ginsburg in San Francisco. The quotes were located for us after an hour interview in which it seemed that the priest talked all around the subject but avoided addressing it directly. Paul and the team were treated to sort of a lecture about karma, enlightened beings, how simply uttering the very name of Lord

Krishna brings great blessings, and how Jesus Christ is now considered one of the Hindu Masters.

I was happy to sit, throughout all of that, in our SUV in the shade, with its doors and windows open, sipping some cold bottled water. I hated to miss the action, especially since it was the very reason I had come, but my stomach had a mind of its own that day and was definitely not cooperating with my higher purposes.

As always, our driver remained vigilant within his vehicle. He didn't speak any English but was pleasant and smiled often. I remarked in Hindi, "Bahot garam hai!" (It's very hot!)

He grinned and replied, "Bahot, bahot garam!" (Very, very hot!)

Having a mild upset stomach during the early days of a visit to India is not at all unusual for Americans and other tourists. It takes time to get adjusted to the Indian diet, and medical preparations are usually advised for travelers, including innoculations.

Some physicians even recommend malaria pills, although I regard that as somewhat of an extreme precaution because malaria is not widely experienced in India, and it seems that malaria pills themselves can often make a person feel sick. For instance, Paul, who came to India with a supply of malaria pills, quickly gave up taking them, because he felt so much better without them.

There are other adjustments for the traveler, too, especially of a dietary nature. Beef-eaters must quickly adapt to either a vegetarian diet or a diet of vegetables, fish and chicken with no beef.

The expression "Holy Cow" originates from India, where the cow is indeed holy, because Krishna was a cow-herd and taught his people to revere the great gifts that come from the cow. In modern American vernacular, one could say that Krishna was a popular cowboy – actually a flute-playing cowboy with a gift for poetry, a knack for attracting the ladies, and a singular, unique gift for conveying the glory of the infinite cosmos and the multi-million year cycles of creation. He is considered a holy personage by Hindus just as Christians revere Christ as the son of God. Similarly, Krishna is considered a form of the ultimate "Godhead" with powers that far transcended his mortal frame. And from Krishna comes the unique Indian reverence for cows.

It is a crime to injure or kill a cow in India. McDonalds restaurants throughout India are vegetarian. Only in predominantly Muslim or Sikh regions (such as Punjab) is beef served in restaurants. In India, the highly regarded gifts of the cow include not only the cow's milk

*The cows rule the roads in India, and it is a crime to injure a cow,
similar to the crime of manslaughter in western countries*

but also the dung, which has many uses, especially as a source of fuel.
Cows are revered and have the rule of the road. They are not fenced
in, and motorists have a legal responsibility to swerve to avoid all cows
that may be wandering on the roads and highways. Better that one
swerve and crash into another car than that one strikes a cow with
one's fender.

One encounters cows on the thoroughfares every single day, and
they might show up anywhere. One could say that they have equal
rights as human pedestrians, at least. And when a cow grows old in
India, they are not sent for the slaughter even then. In a nation where
many elderly human beings are impoverished and uncared for, there
are ample "old age homes" to care for aged cows. But more about that
later, because we actually saw one of the "cow old age homes" later in
our journey.

THE INTERVIEW WITH THE ISKCON PRIEST

I had just finished reading an article about the Rath Yatra festival
at the Jagannath Temple in Puri, when Binny returned. He said the
interview was finished and that it had gone well, and that Paul and
Anil were being shown some of the rare archives of the temple in the

*ISKCON has many luxurious representations of Krishna
covered with gems and jewels of all kinds*

computer data-base. He asked if I would like to come along on a walking tour of the beautiful upper part of the temple. My stomach was
feeling better, and I gratefully accepted the offer. We first went to a
nearby stall and got a cold, orange-flavored soda water for our driver.

After climbing up some long flights of marble stairs on the outside of the temple, we reached the top level. We turned to see a
breathtaking view of the city, spread out below us. The gorgeous flowers and exotic vegetation made the panorama even more spectacular.

As is the custom in many Indian homes and in all of the temples,
we removed our shoes and then stepped inside the ISKCON building.

Paul, Anil, Madhu and DM were standing nearby. We walked with
them to join a slow-moving procession of what looked like several

hundred Indian people strung out in a long line throughout the temple. Huge, colorful paintings of Krishna and many other holy beings of Hinduism adorned the high walls. There was the sense of openness, light and wind, because the temple had many large openings to the outside.

We paid our respects to the deities and then found a sort of gift shop within the temple. Paul bought a collection of beautiful color prints of classical Hindu deities. The prints were stunning and vivid and captured the ancient world of India in all of its glory.

I found a large, brown cotton bag with a wide shoulder strap which I could use to carry my Nikon FM camera and accessories. A bag like that would be functional but modest and not draw attention like an expensive leather camera bag. Above all, one did not want to attract attention while walking around in India in a way that might suggest wealth of any kind. And wealth is all a matter of degree, depending upon where you are. I recalled that in the 1970's, while in Namche Bazaar in Nepal, I encountered three rogues who wanted to kill me to steal the fifty dollars worth of local currency I accidentally revealed in a restaurant. That fifty dollars was actually a thick wad of bills, and unintentionally dropping it from my backpack put my life at risk. Poverty in Asia can be beyond imagining. Yet in some places the wealth can be almost beyond imagining also.

The ISKCON temple projected a level of wealth that was extraordinary, even to those who are used to seeing the glorious interiors of great Christian cathedrals in Europe. This became all the more apparent when we were permitted to enter a part of the temple reserved only for Hindu worshippers. There, our eyes beheld statues of Krishna and Radha that were covered with splendid jewels glistening in the temple's radiant light. The wealth reflected in the display of statues was staggering, and the beauty equally so. A hundred worshippers bowed in respect to the representations of their holy personages.

Upon our return to the van, Paul and Anil described their encounter. The priest, who was the "computer genius" for the temple, was indeed quite young and appeared to be no older than in his mid-twenties. And yet there was no doubt about how devout he was and completely dedicated to the monastic religious life. He made it very clear that the Hindus of ISKCON regard Jesus as one of the holy Avatars of God. They treat Jesus with utmost respect and revere him as they do Krishna, assigning to him in the religious hierarchy the title of Acharya. This is something I think Christians of the west should know. Those who see religions of the east as something alien to their way of thinking can scarcely imagine the extent to which Jesus is revered not only by Hindus but by Muslims. The main argument among these religions would be as to the matter of whether Jesus is in fact "the only begotten Son of God."

On that "technicality," wars have been fought.

On that linguistic dispute, the murdered bodies of millions have been strewn across Europe, Asia and the Middle East throughout the centuries.

The actual transcription of the priest's words are as follows, taken from the transcript of our film **"Jesus in India"**:

"So Jesus is one of the spiritual Masters who is doing this very confidential service for the Lord by bringing so many souls closer to God. So even when Jesus Christ was being crucified, He prayed to the Lord 'Please forgive them. Forgive all these people, they don't know what they are doing.' See, that is the quality of an Acharya. An Acharya or a Spiritual Master is very kind and merciful."

The priest then referred to the teachings of the temple's Spiritual Master, Swami Prabhunanda. He continued: "Our Spiritual Master also says that for twelve years Jesus Christ was in Jagannath, Puri, at the temple of Krishna."

The priest took them to the temple computer room and showed Paul and Anil the temple's vast data storage. The leader of the Krishna Consciousness movement, Swami Prabhunanda, was aware of the channeled writings of Levi Dowling in **The Aquarian Gospel of Jesus the Christ**, which described Jesus' stay at the Jagannath Temple in Puri, India, and the swami confirmed this from his own sources of knowledge but did not identify what those sources were. Were they ancient documents? Were they legends that had been passed down through the generations? It was clear that if more specific information was to be found, it would have to be located at the Hindu Temple of Jagannath in Puri. It was reported to be 2,500 years old, or at least, there had been a Hindu Temple at that site dating back that far even if the current structures had not existed at that time.

That was the site of the headquarters of the Shankaracharya of Puri, a high ecclesiastical office currently occupied by His Holiness Nschalananda Saraswati. At any given time there are four Shankaracharyas (one for each direction of the compass), however His Holiness Nschalananda Saraswati is widely considered the high spiritual leader today of millions of Hindus. He was regarded as being very remote and inaccessible, especially to foreigners seeking information and interviews. However, attaining access to the Shankaracharya remained one of our foremost goals for the journey, as unlikely as it might have seemed at the outset.

Before we ventured onward, Paul asked Anil for a clarification. The priest had repeatedly called Jesus not only by the name Jesus but also by the name Issa. Anil explained that Issa is the name commonly given to Jesus not only by Hindus but also by Muslims. The Koran refers to Jesus as Issa. Also, in **The Secret Life of Jesus Christ**, written by Russian explorer Nicolas Notovitch in the late 1800's, Notovitch explains that Issa is the name that refers to Jesus in the ancient document he was shown at the Hemis Monastery. In fact, that document is called **The Life of Saint Issa, the Best of the Sons of Men**.

Anil said: "Issa comes from Ish, and Ish in Sanskrit is a short form of Ishwara. Ishwara means the Almighty – the all-knowing, omnipresent God, and Masih means messenger or son. So Jesus was called in India Issa Masih or Son of God. Messenger of God."

A GIANT BANYAN TREE

Next, we all drove to a moderately-priced type of Indian restaurant and had a late lunch. We ordered what we wanted, and as always, Binny or Madhu would pay for the meal from our production fund. For me, it was novel not to need money except for souvenirs or personal items. And as for personal items, the most important one was always toilet paper.

I certainly don't mean to be crude, but here is one practicality of life as a tourist in India, especially if you are not staying at the five-star hotels. You often find you need your own supply of toilet paper, and I always kept two or three rolls on hand! Some hotels in India run out of toilet paper, or only give one roll (which can be very small and thin) per room. Sometimes it takes hotel employees one or two hours to bring a fresh roll. I always buy mine at a store and keep it with me to be prepared.

We next drove to a large park which was said to have some of the largest and oldest banyan trees in India. We took a group photo of all six of us on the team standing near a pool of water with some reeds.

Then, thanks to some helpful children, we found what is perhaps the largest and oldest banyan tree in India! It reminded me of stories I had read about the Bodhi Tree under which the Buddha, Guatama Siddhartha, had attained enlightenment.

The time was late in the afternoon; I looked down at my camera and realized I was out of film. I had spare rolls in the SUV and plenty in my luggage. I just looked at the magnificent banyan tree and recorded it forever on the sensitive emulsion of my mind. However, Paul, whose photography skills had entered the digital age, captured the banyan tree for all of us at 5 mega-pixels. There were definitely some disadvantages to ancient forms of photography that rely upon Kodak's film emulsions rather than digital data chips.

Next, we did some filming at sunset outside several large, government buildings which had been built by the British during their era of colonization of India. I was taken aback by a quotation etched in stone across the entire top of one of the buildings. It said: GOVERNMENT WORK IS GOD'S WORK. That was certainly inspired by someone who didn't believe in the separation of church and state.

Binny and Madhu bought some exotic fruit from a street vendor and shared it with me. It was different but definitely tasty!

Dnyanesh Moghe, our associate producer for India and second-unit cameraman, at the giant banyan tree (center with hat)

Paul returned, carrying the camera and tripod, and Anil was with him, and we all piled into the SUV and hastened back to the train station. Anil always did an excellent job keeping us on schedule and aware of the time.

We hired some porters at the train station to help us with our baggage and were soon loaded. The train set out not long after dark and we were on our way to the deep southern part of India --- to Madurai, site of the ancient Meenakshi Hindu Temple, with its thousands of stone statues of Hindu deities in their various forms and incarnations!

One of many train station stops en route to Madurai

3. Southward to the Meenakshi Temple

"For after a man has traveled much,
and suffered much, he thinks back.
Then, he finds pleasures in his pains.
So, I will tell you what you ask
and seek to know."
---*Odysseus in* **The Odyssey** *by Homer*

The train whistle blew loudly as we passed through a village, and I opened my eyes. The sun was just about to rise above the horizon, and I sat up quickly in my clothing, putting on my cowboy boots. They were made of buffalo, American bison, and they had served me well for many years and numerous journeys.

I kept my passport, airline tickets, and other important documents inside a long, sturdy, leather pouch.

On overnight train trips, I put the pouch inside the pillow case, along with my wallet, under my head. Even on bathroom trips, I would take both the leather pouch and my wallet with me. In the daytime, I carried the leather pouch inside my right boot, snug against the left side of my calf. My wallet went in my front right pocket. This helped deter pickpockets.

My original plan, before our documentary filming project began, was to spend two or three days in Madurai. I had wanted to take a series of photographs of the spectacular towers of the Meenakshi Temple complex. I was planning to take many pictures at sunrise, hopefully showing beautiful yellow and orange sky colors at daybreak.

I had heard a legend in several places that at some time young Jesus had taken a break from his studies at the Jagannath Temple at Puri and traveled to visit south India. The legend was that Jesus visited Madurai, among other places. In that ancient time, 2,000 years ago, the sprawling temple complex of today did not yet exist. But tradition has it that there was a noted Hindu shrine there in a grove of trees. Visitors came to the noted places in India from far and wide in those days, principally from China but also from the Middle East. The Silk Road made the journey to India accessible and less arduous than it would have been had there been no such trade.

Hinduism was already thousands of years old in Jesus' lifetime, and some of the learning centers had been in existence for about five hundred years already. As we were to learn later from the Shankara-charya of Puri, the office of Shankaracharya was also about five hundred years old in the days of Jesus. Buddhism also was already well established. It is a credible proposition that anyone during Jesus' lifetime with the kind of devotion to God that Jesus experienced, dedication to reshaping human beliefs (while addressing the psychology of human weaknesses and needs for divine forgiveness) would have had every reason to explore the centers of other great religions of that time. The question at hand, however, was whether in Jesus' case that was true.

In the course of our production, one of the scholars Paul interviewed, a devout Catholic and accredited Vatican journalist named Michael Hesemann (of Dusseldorf, Germany), stated that he had no problem, from a theological standpoint, with the concept of Jesus having visited India. The question for him was determining what was the foundation for believing it. In scholarship, science and archeology there are high standards for determining what is true, or what is probably true. One begins with theory, however, and then comes evidence. In our case, we had a theory based on legend, lore, myth and some evidence. We wanted access to the evidence, and if the ancient evidence could be attained, we hoped that some day it could be scientifically tested. There was a tomb purported by some to be the tomb of Jesus in Kashmir, a tomb of Mary in Pakistan, an ancient manuscript about Jesus in India that had been translated repeatedly by scholars including Nicolas Notovitch and Swami Abhedananda. But that manuscript had not been re-located in modern times. We had much work ahead, and in a sense we felt that we were taking aim at a "lion." There is an old saying in India that it is better to take aim at a lion and miss than to aim at a jackal and kill it. If we did miss, it would be a noble miss. But we were determined not to miss.

Understandably, in our very full filming schedule, my original request for two or three days was crunched into just about twelve hours in Madurai!

This meant an arrival by train about 7:30 a.m. and a departure on another train about 7:30 p.m.

At least I couldn't complain about the weather. It was nearly perfect: clear and sunny with occasional clouds, and no monsoon rains. The temperature was hot but bearable.

The Meenakshi Temple is forbidden to non-Hindus, but our film crew was welcomed. Its many towers are covered with sacred statues.

THE MADURAI RESIDENCY HOTEL

We left the train station with our baggage in two taxis and went to a nearby hotel, The Madurai Residency, on West Marret Street. As always, Sanjay, our travel agent back in Goa, had made the arrangements for us. Although we would be leaving the same day, just after sunset, a room at the hotel would serve as our "base camp." It would be a safe place for us to have our baggage locked up, to use the restroom and shower, or just to take a nap in an air-conditioned room.

The hotel was a bit nicer than where I might have stayed in my old backpacking days. But, a little luxury can be okay! With the help of several hotel employees and the elevator, we soon had all our luggage moved into the room. An Indian gentleman who was either the owner or manager of the hotel had cheerfully walked in with us, pointing out the numerous amenities and services. He mentioned laundry service,

Author Edward T. Martin in the Meenakshi Temple

and we asked, "Could it be ready by around six p.m. today?" He assured us yes, so we quickly made a pile of dirty laundry. Looking at our watches and glancing out the window at the still-good filming weather, we quickly started taking turns in the bathroom to shave and

Director Paul Davids (left) and Producer Anil Kumar Urmil
(right) in the Meenakshi Temple

shower. Others re-checked our camera equipment and re-charged batteries. So, there were six adult members of our filming team, fourteen pieces of baggage, also two single beds (which we wouldn't be using for sleeping), a small table, several chairs, and the door frequently open as uniformed hotel employees came in and out, bringing fresh towels, soap and so on.

Incredibly, the hotel owner remained in the middle part of the room, immaculately dressed in a suit and tie, beaming a big smile and telling how thrilled he was to have such visitors! We thanked him for his help and explained that as soon as we finished taking showers and changing clothes, we quickly had to take taxis to the temple complex for interviews and filming. He never took the hint about leaving the room, so we just walked around him in our underwear, walked over the beds, used blow dryers on our hair and so on. Before too long, we were all ready and trooped out of the room with our camera equipment and the room key.

The hotel owner came behind us, and we asked him to lock the door, which he smilingly did. He meant well! We made a quick exit by elevator and stairs and were soon in taxis, rushing to the Meenakshi Temple Complex.

The three-wheeled taxis of Madurai

A PLACE OF DREAMS

The first time I saw any pictures of the Meenakshi Temple was as a youngster in Texas. I had gone one Saturday afternoon to the Leroy Theatre in Lampasas to see a movie made in 1962 called **"Tarzan Goes to India."** It starred Jock Mahoney as Tarzan, and some of the opening scenes in the movie were views of the Meenakshi Temple towers.

To me, as a kid, it was wildly exotic stuff, and it was made even more so by the knowledge that this was a real place on planet earth. It was a holy place for Hindus, and not a place made for Hollywood. I hoped, as a child, to someday go there and see it myself. And now I was there!

A tower of Meenakshi seen from a nearby street

From several blocks away we could see how magnificent the towers really are.

Our two taxis took us to the entrance area, where we removed our shoes. Our assistant director, Binny, bought our admission tickets. We joined a throng of hundreds of Hindu visitors who were also going into the temple complex. We passed through massive wooden doors and went down stone steps worn smooth into a huge area of hallways with tall, stone columns. Anil went to a side area to speak with some resident Hindu priests to try to arrange filmed interviews.

This was no small feat. For one thing, due to a threatened bombing of the great ancient temple, all filming at the temple had been forbidden as a matter of policy prior to our arrival. Furthermore, to show up on short notice, requesting the attention of the Head Priest of the temple – well, there is an appropriate Jewish word for it, and I think that word is chutzpah. We had no shortage of chutzpah, and we had a determination that was a force to be reckoned with. We were not prepared to hear the word "no," although we were also pragmatists and were willing to surrender if we faced absolutely impossible odds.

Anil worked a miracle that day, as he did many times in our travels. Not only was the ban on video cameras waived for us, but the Head Priest of the temple granted us an interview. We simply had to agree to wait – many hours! They were very busy with weddings, scheduled back to back. Before the sun went down, however, we would have our special opportunity.

A FRIENDLY TEMPLE ELEPHANT

I soon found a friendly temple elephant to visit. This doesn't happen to me very often, so I was taking my time and enjoying the experience. Elephants always remind devout Hindus of one of their most beloved deities: Ganesha, the god of prosperity and good fortune, the remover of obstacles. Ganesha has the head of an elephant, the story being that one time long ago, Ganesha was one of the deity Shiva's children. In a fit of rage, Shiva cut off the head of his son but then felt great remorse. So he placed the head of an elephant on his dead son's body and then brought him back to life. Hindu mythology is strange in many ways to the western mind, because it is so often filled with violent actions (like cutting off the head of a son). But we have only to stop to think of the commandment to Abraham that he sacrifice his son Isaac to realize that the Judeao-Christian heritage is also filled with violence and a jealous and sometimes revenge-seeking God.

Ganesha is a much-admired deity among Hindus, and his image is now known to many in the west. He is a symbol of good luck. And on that fine day, he was certainly the "remover of obstacles" for us.

Paul Davids soon found me and brought good news that I was then hearing for the first time: the temple priests had finally agreed to a videotaped interview later that afternoon! Paul then said, "By the way, I hope that's a tame elephant you're being so friendly with!"

"Yes," I replied, "all temple elephants are known to bestow blessings, and this one is a beauty. Gentle and kind."

The elephant then extended her trunk to the top of Paul's head, giving him a warm, breathy whoof.

Her keeper, standing nearby said, "She is blessing you!"

Director Paul Davids receives a blessing
from the trunk of the temple elephant

We each handed the keeper a coin. I said farewell and patted the sweet pachyderm goodbye. Her keeper smiled and put his palms together in the "namaste" gesture. Paul and I returned the gesture and walked away farther into the long corridors of the temple.

Later, in a dimly lit hallway in another part of the temple, we came across another elephant and its keeper. I almost bumped into it!

I'm glad the temple elephants were so well-behaved and docile. They could easily have crushed someone's foot if they weren't careful, but they were very careful – docile and sweet.

Before long, our whole team got back together in a quiet area just inside the temple's main entrance. Anil told everyone about the scheduled interview that would be coming up late in the afternoon. He suggested that perhaps we all might want to return to the hotel for awhile to escape the heat and take a nap (forgetting for a moment that there were only two single beds). I spoke up and said that if anyone wanted to do that, it was fine with me. But personally, I had come to Madurai to film, and about twelve hours was all we had. Besides, we had good, clear weather, although hot. I said that we have a saying in Texas: "Let's make hay while the sun shines."

Paul chimed in and said that he, too, wanted to make the most of our filming time; we could relax and sleep that night in our berths on the air-conditioned train. Dnyanesh Moghe (DM) agreed also, and so did Binny and Madhu. And so Anil abandoned his thoughts of returning to the hotel, and we enjoyed some cherished hours while waiting in the fascinating temple and also roaming the streets nearby.

A LOFTY VIEWPOINT

Outside the temple, I said that I wished I could go high up, onto the top of a nearby building to do some "aerial photography" of the complex. One of the taxi drivers we had used earlier was standing close by. He said that he knew of an excellent place like that, and they charged no fee!

He quickly drove us over to the building, which I believe was on the west side of the temple complex. A pleasant Indian gentleman wearing a European-type shirt and slacks opened the large glass doors for us.

We trooped in with our two large video cameras, tripods and camera bags. The cold air-conditioning felt wonderful! Around us were a variety of Oriental carpets, Indian clothing, display cases with gold jewelry and so on.

Their business card read: "Meenakshi Treasures, a unit of Cottage Industries Exposition Ltd." Their address was: 30 North Chitrai Street, Madurai, 625 001. Telephone: 91-0452-2630986. The reverse of their card read: **The Balcony on terrace specially made for "AERIAL" Photography of Temple Complex. You are most welcome at anytime; it costs you nothing.**

We were warmly welcomed by several of the employees and were soon taken to the elevator. Perhaps three or four stories up, we reached the rooftop terrace. We stepped out again into the bright sunlight and heat. But the view of the temple complex was spectacular! I think Paul quietly said: "Wow, wow, wow, wow!"

DM and Paul quickly set up the tripods, and with the help of Binny and Madhu, did what is called "white balance" (to calibrate color accuracy) and then began filming. I was actively doing photography with my Nikon FM and also my Vivitar camera, both 35 mm.

Soon, a pleasant gentleman wearing a shirt and slacks arrived. He smiled warmly and gave us the "namaste" greeting with palms pressed together. He then shook hands with everyone and said "Welcome."

I got the impression that he was probably the owner of the business. Then a servant appeared from the elevator with a tray of soft drinks. These were bottles of ice-cold Pepsi Cola; each bottle had a drinking straw. We were delighted with the cold drinks and the owner refused any payment.

They certainly did not refuse payment a short while later, however, when Paul asked to look at various items and then made a purchase of a small medallion in the shape of Ganesha. Paul's independent action, in making the purchase on his own without consulting with Indian members of the crew, inadvertently caused what can only be described as the first moment of ill will that had an impact upon our tight-knit filming team.

In wanting to reciprocate the owner's generosity, Paul had violated an understanding we had made among ourselves that the Indian members of our team would handle all negotiations.

From that moment onward, Paul and I took special care to avoid any direct negotiations and to consult with our Indian friends before making any decisions that involved expenditure of money. Paul found himself apologizing to the others and also trying to be generous with the crew at all times.

The resulting "control" that the crew exercised, in fact, had its greatest impact when it came to our debates about whether it was safe for us to proceed to places of military turmoil in Jammu and Kashmir. Many times they threatened to cut short our filming to protect us from the step of entering potentially dangerous territory. As they put it, they did not want to have our deaths on their conscience, when after all we were essentially in their hands, so far as responsibility for our safety was concerned. Later, this led to occasional clashes and conflict, especially since I was so determined to proceed with everything we had planned, come what may. Fortunately, with efforts from all concerned, we worked out our differences and the filming was not impaired.

I found a bicycle rickshaw driver to take me back to the hotel to get fresh film from my luggage. I was using both Kodachrome 64 color slide film and Kodak color print film. I bought a couple of extra rolls of toilet paper at an air-conditioned shop near our hotel and put

Our local transportation in Madurai was the colorful rickshaw

them in my luggage and then returned to the temple. I continued walk-ing around the outside of the complex, taking pictures until the late afternoon.

Paul, who had been filming outside the temple, and the others went back to the temple headquarters to rendezvous with Anil for the interview with the priests, and I joined them just in time.

It was exciting to at last come face to face with those priests, one of whom was the Head Priest of the temple. I learned that he was very learned and also had a law degree. They led us on a winding, wonder-ful path through sections of the temple we had not yet seen, and DM filmed the entire walk, which is shown in **"Jesus in India."** We even passed another temple elephant.

They took us to a courtyard where there were few people, and we were able to have a private conversation. We asked our questions about the history of the temple and about the legends of Jesus in In-dia. The Head Priest was well versed in all of the lore, which he took to be literal history. He talked about the many people from different cultures, both from the Middle East and from China, who came to Madurai in very ancient times, and he had heard since childhood that Jesus was one of them.

Here is a verbatim transcript of the key points the Head Priest made concerning Jesus in India, including the fact that he had a slight error in describing the ages of Jesus during the Missing Years:

"The gap between the ten to thirty-two years of Jesus Christ, sup-posed to have traveled to India — especially the northern Himalayas, where saintly persons of Hindus are — people who have been living for centuries and centuries. So there He imbibed all the qualities of these saintly-hood people and taken this message of Hindu culture — and He's taken one part of Hindu culture, namely patience, love, affec-tion — because Hindu culture is something very big, very broad. But Jesus has taken that message to western culture and preached it over there. People didn't like it! They actually… what is the word? Ah yes, they actually crucified him. At a later point the people realized that what they had done was a sin, killing a Godly man, and that was when many people began to become Christians."

The Head Priest claimed that the tradition of wearing long hair and a beard was something Jesus had learned from the rishis, or holy men, in India. He claimed that at that time long hair was not a tradi-tion among the Jewish people, apart from the long sideburns or locks worn by Orthodox Jews from early Biblical days. Later in our filming project, Michael Hesemann, the Catholic scholar from Dusseldorf, Germany, contested this by claiming that there were ascetic sects in Judea at the time of Jesus that had rules against cutting one's hair. He believed that during the ages of twelve to thirty Jesus was a member of such a Jewish sect in Judea, a group that devoted their lives entirely to prayer and to following strictly the laws of God.

In stating the claims that Jesus was in India, the Head Priest of the Meenakshi Temple was repeating what we would hear many times in our journey from authoritative figures. These beliefs were clearly an ingrained tradition that went back to ancient times. It was extraordinary to come to understand the great respect Hindus have for Jesus Christ. However, that respect is coupled with the firm belief that Hindus were at least partially responsible for training and teaching Jesus specific devotional and ethical principles, a claim many Christians find very difficult to accept. The deeper I embarked on this research, however, the easier it was for me to accept it, in spite of my Fundamentalist past and my very strict Church of Christ upbringing in Lampasas,

A golden lotus in the pool of water in the center of the Meenakshi Temple complex

Texas. Without question, my years of research and inquiry had brought me to a point of leaving that strict upbringing far behind. I still regarded it with affection, however, and I deeply respected the aspirations and intent of my fellow Texans who still practiced it. I just wished they would become more inquisitive and broaden their knowledge of the world and its history and peoples, instead of being so content to stay within the confines of their small towns without any desire to "look over the next hill to see what's there."

Around sunset, I was back on the rooftop terrace taking more pictures and chatting with the owner. Paul, Binny, and DM were in very high spirits because of what they regarded as a very succesful interview with the High Priest.

Madhu had gone with Anil back to the hotel.

As darkness approached, a dazzling myriad of lights began to turn on within the towers and throughout the temple complex. Paul was shooting and said he was getting some great footage! DM wasn't with him at the time and had left Paul with the second camera, the camera Paul had rented in the U.S. and brought with him to India.

Paul knew right then that he wanted that footage of the Meenakshi Temple at night to be the first shot of the opening title sequence of the movie. Little did we know then that the footage was to become lost – it was the only footage of the entire journey that could not be located when we returned to the United States after six weeks of travel in India. Paul was sick about that. There was nothing else he wanted to use for the background to the opening title of the movie, **"Jesus in India."**

He searched everywhere. Finally, about three months later, he got an extraordinary surprise. Paul had been shooting with the backup camera that he had rented from cinematographer Alex Scott in Los Angeles, an old schoolmate of Paul's son Scott Davids (who is now an accomplished editor and special effects designer in Hollywood for some very major studio films). That night of filming the Meenakshi Temple from the rooftop of "Meenakshi Treasures of Cottage Industries" was the last time that camera was used, and Alex didn't use it for months following its return to him. Paul had searched the camera case before returning that camera to Alex, but no one had thought that the tape might never even have been removed from that camera.

The mystery was solved when Alex Scott located it. He told Paul that he was about to tape over it when he suddenly remembered Paul had told him about the missing tape! And so a very sad story ended up having a very happy ending. You will see the footage Paul filmed that night as the background for the opening titles and main credits of **"Jesus in India."**

I returned to the hotel for a quick shower and then put on fresh clothes and went downstairs to the restaurant. DM had arrived back by then and he joined me for a cold beer in the restaurant. The brand was an Indian beer, Kingfisher, and it was pretty good. I told him the story of how a bottle of Pakistani beer called Murree Beer had been the opening chapter of my first book (a chapter called "A Very Strange Bottle of Beer") and how I had been recollecting that incident in my life for many years. We had a good laugh and were soon joined by Binny who said the filming was over for the evening. Our Indian food soon arrived, and later after our whole team had eaten, we packed our baggage and went in taxis to the train station. Yes, our schedule called for us to take a train out of Madurai that very night!

At the train station, we sat with our luggage on the platform, waiting for our express train to arrive. Even after dark it was still very hot

Worshippers sit cross-legged on the stone floor of the Meenakshi Temple

and uncomfortable. About that time, DM's cell phone rang and he began talking to someone. He stood up, began to pace around, and he seemed upset.

He then walked over to talk quietly with Paul and Anil, and then he returned to where I was and told me his wife, back in Goa, had been injured in a car accident. He would be getting on a different train on another platform to return to Goa immediately. He said he would re-join our team in New Delhi for the last part of our project.

We were all very upset, because we had hoped to have DM with us for the entire journey, but such was not to be. Fortunately, his contributions later on to our filming in Kashmir, when he rejoined us, and footage he took later at the Hemis Monastery in Ladakh and Manali, more than compensated for the fact that he wasn't with us on our many weeks of traveling throughout India.

We shook hands and said farewell. He picked up his baggage and was soon out of sight. DM, our cheerful second cameraman and associate producer for India, was gone, and a much longer journey lay ahead, including a terrible heat wave in Orissa. The hot, still air in Madurai suddenly seemed absolutely oppressive. It was almost beyond comprehension that it could be that hot at eleven p.m. at night.

We boarded the train and sat in silence for a long time, relishing the time we had at the Meenakshi Temple. But I sure could have used another one of those Kingfisher Beers.

En route to Chennai, when daylight came, we all took lots of pictures from the train of the colorful sights along the way, terrain and people and buildings unique to India, unlike sights anywhere else in the world.

Stopped at a train station en route to Chennai

An ascetic walks on the train tracks

*A porter at a rural train station
always carries baggage on his head*

4. On to Chennai, Home of Apostle Thomas

And Vasco da Gama said to the people:
"Who was it that brought you Christianity?"
And they replied: "It was Thomas, the Apostle,
the one you call Doubting Thomas."
---folklore from South India

In the Year of Our Lord, 1498, the Commander Vasco da Gama and his fleet of Portuguese ships and sailors arrived on the Malabar coast of southwestern India. To their amazement, they found thousands of Christian Indians throughout many parts of south India. When they inquired about the origins of the Christian teachings that had resulted in the conversion of so many people in a country so far from the Holy Land, where Christianity was not expected to be found, they were told that none other than the Apostle Thomas, one of Jesus' original twelve Apostles, had come to India and taught their ancestors.

I remembered that I had first heard about Thomas's travels and teachings in India during my first trip to India in 1974. At that time, I was only able to travel and do research in northern India. However, I was told that in southeastern India at the great port city of Madras (now known as Chennai), there is a tomb of St. Thomas and a St. Thomas Cathedral. Also, on the outskirts of Madras at Mylapore, there is a place called St. Thomas Mount which has a chapel and numerous relics claimed to date back to the era of the life of St. Thomas. They also claimed that Mylapore is the place where St. Thomas was martyred in the year 72 A.D.

On that previous journey in 1974, I took notes and decided that on a future trip to India I would make a side trip to Madras and investigate the evidence firsthand. And now at long last, after traveling on the overnight sleeper train from Madurai, here we were in Chennai! A priceless opportunity had arrived for me to learn first hand about the roots of Christianity in southeastern India, a discovery which had astonished the Portuguese explorer Vasco da Gama and his crew.

We paid the train porters, and while Anil and Madhu were arranging for taxis, Paul and I were delighted to see the image of Mahavatar Babaji in the front window of a nearby yellow taxi scooter that was just taking on passengers. We took that as a good omen for a very specific reason! In the teachings of Paramahansa Yogananda, the great Indian sage and friend of Mahatma Gandhi, who became the first major teacher of yoga (after Vivekenanda) in the west, it so happens that the particular type of yoga Yogananda brought to the west (Kriya Yoga) was first taught by Mahavatar Babaji in the Himalayas of India. Babaji, who has a most youthful appearance, according to legend and Yogananda's teachings, is said to be a deathless guru who has lived for centuries in a pure and uncorrupted state. It was on a journey to the Himalayas that a householder and father named Lahiri Mahasaya came upon Babaji over a century ago. Babaji is said to have taught Lahiri Mahasaya the secret technique of Kryia Yoga, an ancient technique for

A photo of a statue of Babaji, the Christlike Yogi of
modern India, in the home of a devotee in Kolkata (Calcutta)

unleashing the hidden powers of consciousness that lie dormant in the spinal column of all of us, through specific methods of breathing and meditation. Yogananda taught that this was the original yoga technique taught by Krishna to Arjuna of the ancient Hindu scripture, the ***Bhagavad Gita***.

Supposedly the technique later was lost for centuries, until Babaji rediscovered it and became custodian of this Hindu holy secret.

A drawing of Babaji from Self-Realization Fellowship.
There are no photos of this yoga master

Applying this technique that he received from Babaji in his daily life, along with great religious devotion to both the father and the mother aspects of God (the Heavenly Father and the Divine Mother, in Hinduism), Lahiri Mahasaya came to be one of the supreme sages of India before the onset of the 20th century. The dialogue between Krishna and Arjuna, speaking of the greatest mysteries of time, creation, the cosmos and the deathless creator, Brahma, is the very heart and soul of the Hindu holy book, ***The Bhagavad Gita***.

It is widely believed in India, among Lahiri Mahasaya's disciples, that he worked miracles, and in ***Autobiography of a Yogi***, Yogananda claims that meditation on a photograph of Lahiri Mahasaya saved his life when he had cholera when he was a boy.

Lahiri Mahasaya, disciple of Babaji

Although Yogananda's father and mother were direct devotees of Lahiri Mahasaya, Yogananda himself learned Kryia yoga and was initiated into its liberating powers by another Hindu sage who became his master or guru, namely Swami Sri Yukteswar.

Swami Sri Yukteswar, guru
of Paramahansa Yogananda

In fact, Sri Yukteswar, who at least into the 1930's had several ashrams (places of Hindu training for new monks and future swamis), told his young disciple Yogananda that Babaji had personally told him that he would send to him a spiritually gifted young man whom Swami Sri Yukteswar would train and some day send to the west, thereby fulfilling Babaji's promise of sending to the western world the ancient secret yoga technique which Krishna taught to Arjuna, and which Babaji taught to Lahiri Mahasaya.

This was a prophecy that was clearly fulfilled in Yogananda's life. Yogananda founded the Self-Realization Fellowship in America, and he established several SRF temples and centers for initiating and teaching Americans Kriya Yoga, first in California and later in other states.

In fact, Paul Davids' home in Los Angeles is located a short distance from the SRF Mother Center, where Yogananda lived and taught and developed SRF from a small organization to one with many adherents throughout the western world. Before embarking on the passage to India, Paul and Anil Urmil had gone to the SRF Mother Center to meditate and silently and respectfully appeal to Yogananda (and the line of Yogananda gurus) for protection on the journey that lay before us.

While this may seem like extensive background, and at first glance may seem far afield of the topic of the Apostle Thomas in India, actually it is not, and the interconnections are meaningful.

Yogananda taught and wrote in his posthumously published two-volume magnum opus, *The Second Coming of Christ: The Resurrection of the Christ Within You*, that Jesus Christ did travel extensively in India. Furthermore, he taught that part of the meaning of the life of Christ is embedded in what he refers to as "Christ consciousness." This is said to be the holy and beatific consciousness that Christ attained.

Yogananda believed that through meditation and devotion, this expanded or "cosmic consciousness" can be attained by any mortal who follows the path of Kriya Yoga. However, Yogananda believed that this attainment of the perfection of Christ consciousness usually takes many lifetimes, in the path of reincarnation long taught in the Hindu religion.

The Gospel of Thomas, the very ancient script quite probably dating to Christ's lifetime which was found at Nag Hammadi Egypt in 1948 (or at least approximately as old as the other accounts of the New Testament, according to the foremost scholar in that field, Prof. Elaine Pagels of Princeton University) gives a far more "eastern" version of Jesus' teachings than is found in the four canonical Gospels of Matthew, Mark, Luke and John.

In fact, there are strong hints in the *Gospel of Thomas* that suggest that it is possible that the original teachings of Jesus were closer to Hindu beliefs than ever assumed in the west, emphasizing that "the Kingdom of God is within you" and "Blessed is the man who comes into being before he comes into being" (reincarnation).

And so, as a result of this background, you may understand that our momentary "sighting" of an image of Mahavatar Babaji in the window of a taxi-cab at the train station took on a larger than life significance for us on this journey. In that image, we saw the supposedly deathless guru who had foretold the journey of Yogananda from India to the west. And now here we were, as scholars investigating these historical interconnections, seemingly greeted by Babaji upon our arrival from America in India's land of Saint Thomas. There was the intuitive sense, for both Paul and myself, of something mysterious "coming full circle" and a special significance in that moment.

Paul and I wanted to stop and film the image of Babaji in the taxi window, but before we could even take a picture of it, that taxi was gone, winding its way out of the parking lot and into the city.

Soon we and the other members of our crew were squeezed into two yellow taxis, along with our abundant luggage, and we continued onward. However, the thought of Babaji lingered in our minds and would have recurring significance later in our travels. There were two other times we saw an image of Babaji in our travels in India, later in Calcutta near the childhood home of Yogananda and in Puri at the ashram of Swami Sri Yukteswar. In our imagination, it was easy to cling to the feeling that perhaps Babaji had, in effect, winked at us that day, and that he was cloaking us in his aura of protection.

With those thoughts coursing through our minds and the bright sunlight of Chennai assaulting our eyes, soon we were all climbing out of those cabs and walking up to our hotel.

After showers and breakfast at our hotel, we all boarded an SUV and headed out to St. Thomas' small chapel in Chennai.

Thank God that vehicle had air conditioning! Not great air conditioning, but at least it played a small role in sparing us, for a short while, from the oppressive heat that was engulfing us. With all our baggage safely at the hotel, the five of us (Paul, Anil, Madhu, Binny and myself) traveled to the southwest outskirts of Chennai to reach the hill known as St. Thomas Mount.

THE MARTYDOM OF APOSTLE THOMAS

I had somehow imagined that the scenery in this part of India might be mostly lush, tropical jungle, but to my surprise, the landscape was semi-arid and reminded me of parts of southern Arizona!

We drove our vehicle up a paved road to the summit of St. Thomas Mount in Mylapore adjoining Chennai (also known as Madras). There, we got out and entered a rectangular yellow building – the St. Thomas Chapel. This was the location of the actual, original chapel where the Apostle St. Thomas, "Doubting Thomas," had preached for many years in India.

What a quirk of fate that we arrived at a time, or a day, when the chapel authorities were simply nowhere to be found. Our desire was to set up our camera on a sturdy tripod and have the freedom to film the interior of this historic building to our hearts' content. En route, we had imagined the likely restrictions we would find. It was not uncommon for guards and authorities to allow visitors with handheld, amateur cameras access to certain historic places, but they usually turn aside anyone with more professional equipment and especially those who use a tripod.

There were no priests or nuns or church authorities present to turn us aside in our mission. A brief conversation between Anil and Madhu and one guard, and of course a donation, resulted in our having entirely free reign.

The opportunity to film inside this church, focusing on all its details, including religious statues, icons and various impressive paintings, including purportedly very ancient relics, was fortunate indeed. Those shots can be seen in **"Jesus in India."**

Although the building itself had been rebuilt since twenty centuries ago, when Saint Thomas preached at that spot, the ground was hallowed and shrouded in both history and legend.

The chapel at St. Thomas Mount, Chennai, India. This is the location of the original church where St. Thomas preached about two thousand years ago.

As filming continued, I walked outside to visit a nearby gift shop and then walked among the trees to a small cafe run by some Catholic sisters. An ancient ceiling fan was creaking softly as I ordered a cold bottle of Pepsi. They served it with a soda straw in the bottle, as always. The summer heat was terrible that day, and sitting in the shade, I found that drinking a cold Pepsi felt very good indeed. I soon walked back and told Madhu about my discovery, and we brought cold drinks for the whole team.

Later, as I walked more among the trees and fed peanuts to some friendly wild monkeys, I found an intriguing sign. It said that St. Thomas had arrived in India aboard a ship in 52 A.D.

Among the religious relics inside the church was an original painting of Mary and the baby Jesus, said to have been given to Thomas by Saint Luke and brought by Luke to India. It was on display framed and sealed behind glass. The legend about that painting fired the imagination. Could it be true? It was startling to contemplate that this painting was unguarded. There were only a few people in the church, and there seemed to be no security whatsoever for preventing the theft of a priceless ancient relic.

Later in our filming project, we would encounter some skeptical opinions of a Catholic scholar, Professor Anthony Tambasco of Georgetown University, who refused to take all these legends literally. He interpreted some of what we saw – including that painting – as being icons to inspire worshippers that were not necessarily exactly what they were purported to be.

For Professor Tambasco, he could not ascribe literal fact to the image of St. Luke handing that painting to St. Thomas, and St. Thomas carting it among his few possessions all the way to India after the crucifixion. However, at the time we were there, it was certainly hard to argue with the inscriptions and plaques that told the details of St. Thomas' ship docking at the port of Cranganore in southwest India.

The sign I was looking at explained that after his arrival in India in 52 A.D., Thomas traveled and taught Christianity throughout south India for the next twenty years. In the year 72 A.D., Thomas was killed by a fanatical Hindu man who speared him from behind. The murder was claimed to have taken place at this very hilltop in Mylapore, which is now called St. Thomas Mount.

We enjoyed the beautiful view from the hilltop. We could see the Indian Ocean a few miles away to the east. Also, we had a sweeping view of the city of Chennai.

As our team walked around the hilltop we photographed some marvelous statues, and at one place we found a white marble plaque commemorating a visit by Pope John Paul the Second to the site in 1984. That visit by Pope John Paul was also something to contemplate – an official acknowledgement by the Pope himself that the claims regarding the religious importance of this site are worthy of reverent acknowledgement by the head of the Catholic hierarchy. "Where there's smoke, there's fire," I always say. I cannot believe that the Pope's visit would have taken place if he did not intend for Catholics to accept the historic reality of St. Thomas' presence here.

After completing our filming session at the hilltop, we looked at our watches and realized we still had time to visit other locations in the vicinity that were connected to St. Thomas' heritage in India: the Cathedral of St. Thomas in Chennai and the adjacent tomb of St. Thomas in the St. Thomas Museum.

AT THE TOMB OF ST. THOMAS

Soon our SUV arrived at a huge and remarkably impressive white building which is the Cathedral of St. Thomas in Chennai. I reverently looked around inside the beautiful church. It was late afternoon, and various local Indian Christians were praying or sitting quietly in the building. There was no air conditioning, but some ceiling fans were turning.

The Saint Thomas Cathedral in Chennai, near the museum with the St. Thomas tomb

I enjoyed looking at the lovely stained glass windows as filming continued. I then found a place outside in the shade of some trees where there was a pleasant breeze. It was unbearably hot that day, like every other day! Binny found me and gave me a plastic bottle of ice cold water as he greeted me with a cheerful smile.

Our film team continued exploring the grounds and nearby buildings as I rested.

Perhaps half an hour later, Binny returned at a brisk pace and said that filming was continuing now at the actual tomb of St. Thomas. I got up and briskly followed him across a parking area and came to another white building behind the cathedral. That building served as a museum for various relics and artifacts concerning early Christianity in India.

One display had a spear-tip claimed to be the actual spear used to murder St. Thomas. Another display had large reproductions of Indian postage stamps honoring St. Thomas.

Truly, the presence of St. Thomas in India had taken root in the culture in many ways and was at the heart of the history of Christianity in this nation. I kept asking myself why this connection of India to the original Christianity goes unacknowledged in the western world. In spite of Pope John Paul II's visit to pay homage at this spot, most western Christians seem to be quite ignorant of this aspect of Christian history.

And given the foundation of this part of Christian history in India, connected to St. Thomas, it certainly seemed all the more feasible that our speculations and research about Jesus in India could have solid historical basis. We just had to keep probing.

Binny led me to the basement level which has white marble walls and a small chapel. And, in the front area was the tomb of St. Thomas!

The tomb itself was a white marble and glass sarcophagus which contains what looks like a wax figure of Thomas lying in repose, purportedly above the actual remains of the Apostle. As a Christian, the very thought of this took my breath away.

I glanced across the room. Nearby on one wall was a three-dimensional diorama that depicts the martyrdom of Thomas.

Several Indian Christians were sitting quietly in the chapel.

A painting by Caravaggio on another nearby wall (*The Incredulity of St. Thomas*) depicts the resurrected Jesus appearing to the Apostles while "Doubting Thomas" is garishly poking a finger into the wound

where Jesus was pierced by the Roman soldier's spear during the crucifixion.

HOLY GROUND

I remember having a profound and somber feeling as I stood near
the tomb. Could this really be the final resting place of the Apostle
Thomas, one of the original twelve Apostles chosen by Jesus himself?
And if so, why do we hear almost nothing about this in Europe and
the Americas?

Could part of the answer be that if people in the west were made
aware of the evidence of St. Thomas in India, that would open the
flood gates for scholarly examination of all of the evidence for Jesus in
India?

If St. Thomas could get here, why not Jesus?

I began reading a brochure given out by the church entitled: *Santhome Cathedral Basilica, A Quick Introduction.* I quote several paragraphs:

You are standing on holy ground which contains the tomb of St.
Thomas, one of the twelve Apostles (that is, closest associates) of Jesus Christ. He came to India in the year 52 A.D., preached on the west
coast and here, died in this city in 72 A.D. and was buried in Santhome. The Basilica that you are visiting stands over his tomb. In fact,
the Basilica is so constructed that the smaller of its two towers stands
exactly over the tomb of St.Thomas. There is also the shrine where the
next most famous missionary to India, Saint Francis Xavier, used to
pray. You are in the long line of pilgrims and visitors who have been
coming here for nearly two thousand years.

From his many followers, Jesus chose twelve to be his close col-
laborators and gave them power to preach and heal. These twelve are
called "Apostles." Thomas is one of them. He is mentioned four times
in the New Testament of the Bible (the Gospel according to Saint
John). Of these accounts, the most quoted is the one of Jesus' apparition to the other eleven after his Resurrection, when Thomas was ab-
sent. Thomas refused to believe that Jesus had appeared to them. He
insisted: "Unless I see the marks of the nails in his hands, and put my
hand into the wound in his side, I will not believe." During his next
apparition, Jesus called Thomas to him and invited him to check his
wounds. Thomas burst into an act of faith, proclaiming 'My Lord and
My God!'

When the Apostles dispersed to preach in different parts of the world, Thomas left for Parthia and India. His stay and preaching in North and South India are mentioned in two well-known books, **The Acts of Thomas** (Acta Thomae) and **The Teaching of the Apostles** (Didascalia Apostolorum). The great Christian writers of the fourth century, like St. Ephraem, St. Gregory Nazienzen, St. Ambrose and St. Jerome, unhesitatingly affirm the apostolic activity of St. Thomas in India.

The Syrian Christians of Kerala strongly maintain the tradition, handed down from generation to generation in their churches and families, that their forefathers were converts of this Apostle. According to this tradition, the Apostle landed in Kodungallur (Cranganore) in Kerala around the middle of the first century of the Christian era (probably 52 A.D.) and founded Christian communities at several places, like Kodungallur (Cranganore), Niranam, Kollam (Quilon), Palayur, etc. Then he traveled to the eastern parts of the country as far as Mylapore and perhaps even beyond, as far as China. On returning to Kerala, he appointed some of his converts as leaders of the communities that he had founded earlier. Proceeding once again to the eastern parts of South India, he was killed somewhere near Mylapore and buried in that town in 72 A.D. (There are two other sacred spots associated with Saint Thomas in the city of Chennai: SAINT THOMAS MOUNT on the outskirts of the city, where he suffered martyrdom, and LITTLE MOUNT near Saidapet, which has a cave where, according to tradition, the Apostle used to hide and pray.)

The tomb itself was officially opened four times, according to written records we have. As for the church, that too has much history.

Theodore, a sixth century visitor from Europe, spoke of the Santhome church as "a church of striking dimensions, elaborately adorned and designed." The world-renowned traveller from Italy, Marco Polo, travelled here in 1292 A.D. and speaks of it in his journals.

We have reports of this church by Oderic of Podenone (Papal legate) in 1325, by John de Marignolli in 1349, Nicolo de Conti, another Italian visitor, between 1425 and 1430.

However, when the Portuguese arrived in Mylapore in 1517, and again in 1521, they found the Santhome church in ruins, except for the small chapel which contained the tomb of St. Thomas. They rebuilt the church, but on a smaller scale, in 1523. This church became a parish in 1524. It lasted up to the end of the nineteenth century.

In 1893, under Bishop Henrique Jose De Silva of Mylapore, this structure was demolished and the present church built, keeping the tomb of St. Thomas at the heart of the structure. The smaller tower is exactly over the tomb.

NORTHWARD TO ORISSA

We made a donation to the St. Thomas Museum and thanked the gracious people who showed us around. We then got back into our SUV and made our way back to Hotel Central Tower on Poonamallee High Road near the Central Train Station in Chennai.

After we all had a good dinner, Binny walked with me to a nearby shop where I bought a couple of bottles of Kingfisher Beer, which I took back to the hotel room and enjoyed that night with Paul.

After breakfast the next morning, we departed in two taxis to the train station where we boarded an express train for a very long journey northward along the eastern coast of India. We were headed to the capital of the state of Orissa: Bhubaneshwar!

It was a very long, hot train journey, as we traveled northward up the east coast of India. Paul Davids and I were fortunate to have first-class train tickets (which meant we had air conditioning, of sorts, in the sleeper class).

Through one of the only snafus in advance planning, our Indian film team, unfortunately, ended up in the non-air conditioned rear part of the train. It was in the shade, at least, and windy, although they later told us that the wind felt like it was coming from an oven! Some cold bottled water did help, and people fanned themselves to survive.

As our express train barreled through the heat wave in the blazing sunlight, the "air conditioning" at times seemed pretty wimpy! Well, it was a lot better than outside. I sipped on a bottle of cold water and often read one of my India guide books. I always enjoyed looking out the windows at the passing scenery of vast fields and the distant hills of the eastern ghats.

On that train going up the Indian coast, we were the only non-Indian passengers in our area, and Paul often drew quite a crowd of spectators on the train when he put on one of his magic shows to pass the time on the long ride! I always enjoyed the shows, also. I still can't figure out how Paul does most of the tricks!

As I've mentioned before, Paul is an accomplished magician, very skilled at sleight-of-hand and other tricks. He has been a member of the Magic Castle in Hollywood (a professional magician's society and private magical entertainment club) since 1986, back in the days when he was production coordinator of **"The Transformers"** daily animated TV show. Paul had the good fortune to learn sleight-of-hand and other magic techniques from the time he was a boy of thirteen (taught by Philip and "Bobbo" Goldberg of Florida, who were involved with early stop-motion animation filming experiments with Paul), and then the culmination of his tutelage came one summer in Cincinnati when he studied clarinet at the Cincinnati Conservatory of Music. It was there that he met Merelet the Magician, who after seeing Paul perform a magically arranged demonstration of mental telepathy (a trick!), took Paul into his confidence. Merelet showed Paul the great stage illusions and many techniques, swearing the then-sixteen year old young man to eternal secrecy. Ever since, Paul has often carried around a deck of cards (which you actually get to inspect… most of the time) in his pocket, so he can do impromptu performances for friends.

As the end of the day came aboard our train, we were then treated to a larger array of magic from nature - the sunset was spectacular, with glowing colors of orange, yellow and red. Lights would flicker on in distant villages, and soon darkness was gathering.

The train ride to Bhubaneshwar was hotter than an oven

Our attendant soon walked through our train car, taking orders for chicken biryani with rice, for a modest fee. These meals, delivered later in a cardboard box, were always tasty and safe. And a paper cup of tea or coffee always topped off the meal.

Another attendant came through later with clean cotton bed-sheets, a thin, grey wool blanket and small pillow for each adult passenger. There were three narrow bunks on one side, facing another three narrow bunks on the other side, in each compartment. The open end of the compartment faced the aisle, which runs the length of the train car.

The other end of the compartment was a window in the side of the train, with a small folding tabletop underneath. Small, sturdy metal ladders were attached near the aisles, to help people climb into the upper bunks.

I sometimes told Paul that the constant rocking and swaying motion of the train actually helped me to sleep pretty well. He found that hard to believe!

ARRIVAL IN BHUBANESHWAR

We arrived in Bhubaneshwar, the capital of the state of Orissa, about 10 o'clock at night. The heat wave was still in full force, and the high humidity made the heat feel oppressive, even at night.

We arrived in two taxis with all our baggage, pulling up to a government state house. From what we could see of the grounds, the facility looked spacious, with many gardens and few other visitors.

Rajesh Parida, who was one of our local production coordinators, arranged for us to be guests of the State of Orissa and to have rooms at the Statehouse guest quarters.

We had just unloaded our baggage from the taxis when a young reporter arrived from a local television station. Rajesh had tipped him off about our arrival.

Paul and I diplomatically declined to be interviewed and asked for no publicity. We felt it was essential we keep a very low profile the entire time we were in India. If we had attracted attention it would have been all the more difficult for us to gain access to places we wanted to film and to get interviews with the people we wanted to meet. Stories about film productions, even a small one such as ours, spread quickly throughout India in the media, as soon as "the cat is out of the bag." We helped Rajesh understand that, for the success of

Edward T. Martin (left) and Paul Davids (right)
sweating through a production meeting at Bhubaneshwar

our project, our cat had to "stay inside the bag," at least until we were close to completion of the film.

We could easily imagine, at that time, that if the public and perhaps even authorities became aware of the purpose of our undertaking, we could easily have found the obstacles increasing all around us. Controversy is not often welcomed. There are plenty of barriers in this kind of work, without taking a chance of inviting more. We thanked the reporter for his interest and cooperation in NOT writing anything about our visit, and then everyone headed off to sleep.

Our room attendant turned on a complicated sequence of about four switches to get our air conditioning going. There was great suspense as to whether it was even going to work. Finally, it did, and it felt ice-cold and just great!

I went into the bathroom, took a quick shower (from two faucets in the wall and a bucket), dried off, put on my pajamas and got into my twin bed. Paul climbed into the twin bed alongside. He was soaking wet from sweat and asked that we turn off the air conditioning. Outside, it was still as hot as a furnace. Reluctantly, I turned the switch off. Before long, we decided to turn it back on, as the room began to feel like a sauna. The switches refused to cooperate! No matter what

The film crew members were guests
at the state guest house in Orissa

we tried, nothing worked, and our room attendants were sound asleep! Exhausted, I fell asleep anyway.

The next morning, our attendants brought us a light breakfast of hot tea and toast with jam, and they got our air conditioning going!

Anil and the rest of our Indian film team soon lined up a driver with an air-conditioned SUV to meet us. By then, we had the camera battery packs charged up and everything set to go. We were headed for the nearby coastal city of Puri and the legendary Jagannath Temple!

Paul and I reached the SUV first with our equipment, and Paul sat at the very back of the vehicle. We both learned an important lesson in caution, because after Paul sat down, I flipped down a folding seat. The hinged seat was heavy and thudded down with a metal part which slammed hard against the metal floor. Paul's feet were both safe and clear, but just barely so, and it gave us a scare. A few inches, and one of his feet or both could have been crushed. Safety devices are sometimes non-existent in India, and we quickly learned to be extra-careful to avoid injuries!

Our SUV driver soon arrived, started the engine and turned on the air conditioning. Thank God! The reader may be exhausted from reading my hyperbole, again and again, about how hot it was in India that summer. All I can say is, better you read about it than experience it first hand. There are far better times of the year to visit India than June and July.

Binny arrived with a large plastic bottle of water for me. And it was partially frozen! It sounds silly, but with the terrible heat outside, I was delighted to have my own bottle of ice-cold water with big chunks of ice floating in it! It was heavenly! Perhaps you would have had to be there to really understand and appreciate such simple things. But be grateful that you weren't.

TO THE HOLY CITY OF PURI

Soon, our filming team of five, with our driver, was barreling down the two-lane paved road to the coastal city of Puri. We were speeding by a vast number of coconut palm trees and rice fields as we checked our equipment and notepads.

At one place we stopped briefly to drink some fresh coconut milk and take a breather. A boy with a sharp knife hacked open the coconuts for us and even gave us straws. Some local villagers walked past, herding their water buffaloes, while the occasional motorcycle or bicycle sped by.

We soon arrived in Puri and saw the white sand beaches and the pounding waves of the Indian Ocean. Excitement was building, because we knew we were now in the vicinity of Jagannath, which was "world famous" as an "ancient" temple even in the days of Jesus.

Surely young Jesus would have heard of its existence. And surely, for a young man of his holy intent, even from afar – four thousand miles from what we now call the Holy Land – it would have held a certain mystery and allure. Could Jesus have passed his days on earth without ever having heard of it or having the desire to see it?

Coconut milk awaited us with one slice of the boy's machete

5. In Puri and the Jagannath Temple

"Three things cannot be long hidden:
the sun, the moon, and the truth."
---Buddha

When the Russian explorer Nicolas Notovitch was first shown the document, ***The Life of Saint Issa, The Best of The Sons of Men***, he quickly realized its profound importance. The age of the document he saw at the Hemis Monastery at 14,000 feet elevation in Ladakh, India, was uncertain. It was in Tibetan and probably not more than about three hundred years old. However, he was told that it was a translation of the original copy that was two thousand years old in the Pali language, and that it dated to within a couple of years following the crucifixion of Jesus Christ – that it was written soon after the crucifixion and recorded highlights of the life of Jesus, including details of the eighteen "Hidden Years" from ages twelve to thirty.

The year that Notovitch was shown the document was 1887. At the time, Notovitch, a Russian-born Jew who had converted to Christianity, was on a lengthy expedition throughout India and the Himalayan regions.

In northwestern India, in the province of Ladakh, he visited the Hemis Monastery for a short duration and knew nothing of ***The Life of Saint Issa*** when he had first departed to return home. However, soon after leaving, he was thrown from his horse and suffered a broken leg. There was no hospital nearby, so he was taken back to Hemis Monastery to recuperate.

After several weeks, according to Notovitch's account of his travels, the Buddhist monks grew to know and trust their visitor from Russia enough to tell him about the ancient document concerning Jesus in India.

With the help of the monks, constantly questioning them about the meaning of each word and phrase, Notovitch was able to translate the document to his native Russian, carefully writing down the translated text. Later, after returning to Europe, Notovitch translated the text into other languages as well.

He showed the text to officials at the Vatican and to other experts. Many people downplayed the importance of the document, refusing to assign credibility to it or to Notovitch's story of his travels.

Time and again, he was advised not to start trouble by disseminating the information. One Oxford professor, an expert in various Oriental languages named Dr. Max Mueller, launched a smear campaign against Notovitch.

Mueller played the role of notorious debunker, attacking Notovitch personally, detracting from Notovitch's reputation and honor as a writer.

His accusations, which with the benefit of the hindsight we have today seem in some respects to have been wild and even ludicrous. Those accusations took many twists and turns. He claimed Notovitch had never even been to the Hemis Monastery or Ladakh (later disproved by records of a visit Notovitch made to a dentist in Ladakh). He also accused Notovitch of concocting the story and the document to try to clear the Jews of any guilt or blame for Jesus' crucifixion by placing the blame entirely on the Romans.

Once again, logic and the passage of time reveal the motivations of Mueller's tactics, especially since we know for a fact today that other men with esteemed reputation were also shown the same document at Hemis in the decades that followed, and it was re-translated about thirty years later with only subtle linguistic differences.

In my research and in my quest, I was of course tantalized by the possibility that **The Life of Saint Issa** perhaps could still be found at the Hemis Monastery, but that it might genuinely have been exactly what Notovitch claimed: a translation into the Tibetan language from a two thousand year old holy script in the Pali language.

It didn't seem unreasonable to me that such a text, written by a visitor from India who was in the Holy Land at the time of the crucifixion, would have placed the blame for the execution of Jesus entirely on the Romans. The details of the political maneuvers that led to the condemnation of Christ would likely have been unknown to an observer unfamiliar with such details and with no access to such information, claims and accusations.

I had long assumed that if Notovitch's claim were true, and the missing document he had translated was genuine, then there should be some supporting evidence for some of its claims and details. Among those "trails of evidence" is the fact that one part of the writing specifically tells that young Jesus was a student at the Jagannath Temple (at the seaside city of Puri in the state of Orissa) in northeastern India. And this was where we had arrived, a short while after our drink of that coconut milk. What evidence would we find here? Was there any possibility we could obtain an audience with the Shankaracharya, which would be similar to a non-Catholic obtaining an audience on short notice with the Pope?

Since the early years of my research on this subject, I have been tantalized by the fact that a separate document, *The Aquarian Gospel of Jesus Christ* by Levi Dowling (a chaplain in the Union Army during the American Civil War), gives the same information about young Jesus at the Jagannath Temple that is found in the purportedly ancient manuscript Notovitch translated at the Hemis Monastery, half a world away from anyplace Levi Dowling had ever visited.

How could Levi Dowling have come by such information? His claim is that his book was "channeled" by accessing the so-called Akashic Records.

Legend has it that the Akashic Records are a sort of spiritual or cosmic repository of all events and all knowledge, and that some mystics have tapped into this repository in trance states and have come by valid information they could not possibly know from any other source.

Skeptics may have a field day with claims about the Akashic Records. Nevertheless, the overlap of information in the Dowling Book and Notovitch's translation of the Hemis text is quite puzzling, because it is virtually certain that neither man ever heard of the other. There is no evidence that I have been able to find that Dowling ever had access to *The Life of Saint Issa*, which took many years to circulate in the United States after its original release in Europe.

Similarly, there is no evidence Notovitch ever heard of the Union Army soldier in America named Levi Dowling. How then can a logical mind account for the fact that both men were claiming Jesus of Nazareth spent time at the Jagannath Temple in Puri?

Therefore a large and looming question during our journey was: what would authorities at Jagannath, today, say about Jesus in India? Specifically, what would the Shankaracharya, one of the four ecclesiastical heads of modern Hinduism, who presides at the Jagannath Temple, have to say about such claims? Could access to such an authority ever be gained by our film crew? If so, we knew it would be truly historic. And fate or divine providence (take your pick) was soon to reward our efforts.

Notovitch's story, including the complete translation of ***The Life of Saint Issa, the Best of the Sons of Men***, is included in his book: ***The Unknown Life of Jesus Christ*** by Nicolas Notovitch, published by Tree of Life Publications, Joshua Tree, California. Sections of that purportedly ancient manuscript are reproduced at the end of Chapter Twelve, preceding the Afterword written by Paul Davids.

RATH YATRA

Once a year, at a special celebration called "Rath Yatra", holy Hindu images of various incarnations of Hindu deities are placed on huge wooden carts and rolled long distances. Huge throngs of devout Hindus crowd together near the Jagannath Temple for these occasions.

During the 1700's and 1800's, British soldiers attended these events. Some observers claimed that over-zealous Hindus sometimes threw themselves in front of the rollers and were crushed to death because the gigantic floats would never stop for man or beast. Thus, the expression "rolling like a juggernaut" entered the English language and came to mean "an unstoppable force."

It happened for us by chance (or divine order) that when our filming team arrived at Puri, the final preparations for the Rath Yatra festival were taking place. What a sight! And what a vast number of Hindu pilgrims!

Rajesh Parida (left), production coordinator in Puri,
with his mother and father at Rath Yatra Festival preparations

A cart being completed for the Hindu Rath Yatra Festival at Jagannath

There were huge crowds of people everywhere, because the annual Rath Yatra festival of Jagannath was about to begin.

In fact, pilgrims from all over India were arriving in large numbers by the hour. It was around the third week in June, and the Orissa heat wave was intense! The temperature was about 110 degrees to 115 degrees Fahrenheit --- and the humidity made it feel worse! It was definitely not the "dry heat" one experiences when the temperature reaches the same range in a southwestern American city such as Phoenix.

We checked into our hotel – which looked pretty spartan – and cranked the air conditioning to the high setting. After leaving our baggage safely, we locked our rooms and headed out again to our vehicle.

On the first day, we saw the preparations for Rath Yatra, the building of the huge carts.

During the day, to our great excitement, word came to us that we had been granted an appointment with His Holiness the Shankaracharya of Puri. We had been told that the Shankaracharya never gives interviews, but we had a representative ask. When His Holiness heard the purpose of our interview, he said "Yes".

Even throughout the next morning, we believed we would not be able to film the interview. We also believed it was likely that Paul and I would not be permited a direct audience with the Shankaracharya, only our Indian representatives and Indian producer, Anil Urmil, would meet the Shankaracharya. We were led to believe that it was unlikely even Anil would be allowed to have a picture of himself taken with the Shankaracharya, which if true would deny us any evidence that we actually were there!

Our team arrived outside the courtyard area of a building adjacent to the Jagannath Temple. Non-Hindus are not allowed in the temple itself, so our interview would take place in a different building.

We sat down on the stone steps in a shady area and removed our shoes. A pleasant Hindu priest asked us to stand up so he and another young man could frisk everyone. After that, servants brought us ice-cold bottles of Pepsi on trays, with a drinking straw in each bottle. Of course the heat was still sweltering, even in the shade, but I felt a little better.

Upon our arrival at the compound of the Shankaracharya, our Indian team explained at length to the Shankaracharya's advisors the purpose of our visit and of our film. It was also explained that our director, Paul Davids, should be considered a devotee of the great Indian sage Paramahansa Yogananda, as Paul had studied Yogananda's teachings for many years and had read Yogananda's books and had even meditated at Yogananda's Los Angeles Mother Center.

Thus, it was decided that Paul would be treated as "an honorary Indian" and "honorary Hindu" for this visit, and I soon learned that I would not be excluded from attending the interview, either.

The greatest moment was when we were instructed to bring in our camera to film the interview, which would be conducted in Hindi between Anil Urmil and the Shankaracharya.

Soon we were all escorted into a building and up the stairs into a spacious room. Windows and doors were open to the outside air, and ceiling fans creaked softly as they whirled. No furniture was in the room, only colorful cushions on the floor. A small, raised platform was at one end of the room, with a large cushion.

We all sat cross-legged on the floor and waited. I was sweating profusely because of the heat and humidity. I fanned myself with a paper I was holding.

After several minutes, a side door opened and His Holiness, the Shankaracharya, Swami Nischalananda Saraswati, entered. As previously instructed, we all stood up and bowed. He smiled, returned the bow, and sat down calmly at the cushion on the platform. His Holiness Shankaracharya Nischalananda Saraswati was elderly but lively,

Distant dome towers - the Hindu Jagannath Temple, ancient and modern

with a short, white beard and mustache and white hair. He wore the orange robes of a holy man and had a dignified demeanor.

Unfortunately, we were not allowed to use our "shotgun microphone," as it is called, the lengthy parabolic microphone which sits atop the camera and to some might look threatening. It was not possible to use a lavalier microphone (pinned to clothing) either, and furthermore, we had to keep some distance between ourselves and the Shankaracharya.

Two other complications affecting our sound were the noisy ceiling fans, and the fact that a door behind the Shankaracharya was left opened, because of the heat.

All of this played havoc with our sound recording. Fortunately, it "squeaked by" and was useable, and the words of the Shankaracharya can be heard and discerned by those who speak Hindi. It took a lot of help from a Hollywood sound studio, about one year later when we were in post-production, to amplify and clarify the sound of the Shankaracharya's voice, and it is still not really satisfactory and is one of the only disappointments in the film. Nevertheless, the words can be heard and have been translated in subtitles.

RESEARCH BY DR. JIM DEARDORFF

Several years before my arrival "at the feet of the Shankara-charya," I learned that Nicolas Notovitch and Levi Dowling were not the only sources whose research and writings placed young Jesus at the Jagannath Temple. Paramahansa Yogananda also taught of this. Knowing of my intense interest in all of this, Dr. Jim Deardorff, a professor at the University of Oregon with a background in meteorology and a strong personal interest in the history of religion, frequently sent me clippings and articles and letters related to Jesus in India.

I will quote several paragraphs here from Professor Deardorff's correspondence with me, which he excerpted from p.16 of *Self-Realization Magazine*, winter, 1992, a publication of Paramahansa Yogananda's organization.

The article is by Sri Daya Mata, who personally worked with Yogananda for the last decades of his life, and who now heads the Self-Realization Fellowship. When she speaks of the Shankaracharya, she is referring to the previous Shankaracharya of Puri, who held that office prior to the current Shankaracharya. She writes:

"In 1959 I discussed this (Jesus being in India during the 'unknown years') with one of India's great spiritual leaders, His Holiness Sri Bharati Krishna Tirtha, the Shankaracharya of Puri. I told him that Guruji had often said to us that Christ spent some of his life in India, in association with India's illumined sages. His Holiness replied, 'That is true. I have studied ancient records in the Puri Jagannath Temple archives confirming these facts. He was known as "Isha" or "Issa," and during part of his time in India he stayed in the Jagannath Temple. When he returned to his part of the world, he expounded the teachings that are known today as Christianity.'

"In the above, 'Guruji' refers to the yogi Paramahansa Yogananda. Puri is a city in northeast India on the coast, where the Jagannath Temple is located. The lost years verses (found by Notovitch and others) say that Issa had spent time at this location. So, Bharati Krishna Tirtha has apparently actually studied from the ancient records there at the temple, which tell of Isha having been there, back in the early 1st century. Yogananda has authored many books, and in his ***The Divine Romance*** (1986) one may read (p.257) that he was indeed well aware of the lost years evidence."

Professor Deardorff continues in his correspondence to me:

"The only part of Sri Tirtha's above statement I would contest is that the teachings of Christianity reflect at all accurately what Isha, alias Jesus, taught in Galilee and Judea. Instead, I see Christianity as reflecting most accurately what St. Paul taught, not what Jesus taught."

(This ends the statement from Dr. Jim Deardorff.)

OUR AUDIENCE WITH THE SHANKARACHARYA

As I stated previously, Anil conducted the session in Hindi, thanking His Holiness for granting the interview and then asking a series of specific questions. My own fluency in the Hindi language is very limited, as I've said, but I could sometimes understand the gist of what was being discussed.

Here is the translation of the interview, subsequently done by Anil, of the actual interview as it appears in the film **"Jesus in India"** and printed here with permission.

SHANKARACHARYA:

I am the 145th Shankaracharya. Actually this tradition is 5000 years old from the era of Sat Yuga. During the rapid spread of Buddhism, this tradition was suppressed. The first Shankaracharya was born in 506 BC. The Jagannath Temple was established as an education center in 483 BC.

ANIL KUMAR URMIL:

In the Christian New Testament there is hardly any mention of Jesus' life from age 12 to 30. When Ed Martin asked about the Missing Years in his church, he was silenced.

SHANKARACHARYA:

The truth was submerged to propagate lies. Many important religious figures have come here to study. Jesus Christ also came here to study.

ANIL KUMAR URMIL:

So it is true He came here to study?

SHANKARACHARYA:

YES, YES!

ANIL KUMAR URMIL:
So Jesus Christ DID study here for a few years?

SHANKARACHARYA:
He studied the Achar Samhita — the Code of Conduct. He must have met the Shankaracharya of that time.

ANIL KUMAR URMIL:
Are there any ancient texts that have a record of this?

SHANKARACHARYA:
Our ancient records were buried someplace here to protect them from invaders. That is why they are hard to find today. And even though we know these things, the Christians are not willing to believe it. Jesus studied our teachings of Truthfulness, Mercy, Charity, Serving Others, Compassion and Ethics. The fact that Hindus made a contribution to Jesus' learning is not accepted by some people.

ANIL KUMAR URMIL:
It is a fact that our very ancient Hindu text, the Bhavishya Maha Purana has an account of King Shalivahana meeting Jesus in Kashmir, India.

SHANKARACHARYA:
Yes, that is true, but the Christians will still not believe it. Christians know Jesus was missing for many years. Where was He? Where was He living? Where was He traveling? He lived in Kashmir. Traveled all over India. The truth has been covered up.

And so, His Holiness was certain in his own mind – without any doubts – that young Jesus had been a student there, at the Jagannath Temple. However, he did not affirm that he himself had seen ancient written documents in the temple archives which confirm it. When asked about that, he referred to the records as having been hidden in previous eras to protect them from invaders.

The question remains: does this mean that the records which support what the Shankaracharya said cannot be found and could never be produced "in evidence"? Or was the Shankaracharya avoiding a direct answer, because for whatever reasons, he did not wish for anyone to attempt to convince him or pressure him to produce the records?

I found myself wondering whether perhaps there was a "behind the scenes" tacit understanding between the world's religious leaders that no religion would produce any "smoking gun" to undermine the teachings and dogmas of any other.

After all, according to *Self-Realization Magazine*, the previous Shankaracharya had stated to Sri Daya Mata, unambiguously, that he had seen the ancient records at the Jagannath Temple that confirmed these claims. In fact, at that later stage of his life, he expressed the intent to write a book that would have included this, but as fate or divine providence would have it, he passed away before the book was written.

In other parts of the interview, the current Shankaracharya implied that, for political reasons and reasons of the power structure of various religions, today the status quo is favored by the power structure – favored above and beyond any discoveries that could tip the "balance of credibility" among the world's major belief structures.

Religion, he said, is big business, and because of huge amounts of money involved, the real historical truth often takes a back seat to modern pronouncements that have ulterior motives and spin. Just think about the politics that were involved when the Dead Sea Scrolls were discovered, and how long it took, how many decades, before they left the exclusive domain of a tight-knit group of scholars and entered the public domain.

The interview continued for at least twenty minutes. We all thanked His Holiness and made the "namaste" gesture of blessing with our hands before departing. His Holiness left through the same door through which he had entered. We collected our filming equipment, content that we had made a breakthrough. Though it might take a few years for the world to appreciate it, getting an interview of that nature with someone of that stature within India was historic and unprecedented.

We talked for awhile downstairs in the courtyard, surrounded by some of the young trainee Hindu priests. Some of those boys seemed scarcely twelve or thirteen years old, and already they were set on a path for future positions of importance within the Hindu world.

As I looked around at those boys, I tried to imagine how it would have been for young Jesus, arriving at Jagannath at perhaps fourteen or fifteen years old. The Notovitch documents claimed that Jesus studied here and then rebelled, became a troublemaker because he wouldn't accept the strictures of the caste system and the treatment of the lower castes as inferiors. It went against his core principals that all of us are children of the Heavenly Father and made in the Father's image. He became so unpopular, or so goes the story, that he had to escape to save his life, as an assassin was sent to kill him.

How very much in character those stories are, for the person we think of as Jesus Christ. It brings to mind images of Jesus in the temple in Jerusalem, throwing over the tables of the money-changers.

It was almost sunset, and we drove for a long distance on the road beside the white sand beach and the pounding ocean waves.

AT THE SUN TEMPLE OF KONARK

The next morning we got up very early, in the pre-dawn darkness, to drive about thirty miles to visit the Konark Sun Temple, northeast from Puri. Once we arrived there, Paul, Anil, and Madhu diligently trooped off with the camera and tripod to scout some good shooting locations. Binny and I first needed some strong tea and a breakfast pastry.

The Sun Temple of Konark

We found a vendor with a tea stall under a banyan tree. While Binny and I were sitting and enjoying our tea in the growing sunrise, a small group of friendly monkeys walked up. I gave them some pastry pieces and we were amused by their antics.

Everywhere in India, monkeys are treated with respect and affection because of the great love of Hanuman, the monkey deity who has the head of a monkey and the body of a man.

Hanuman is one of the principle characters of the great epic poem, **The Ramayana**. This, like the **Bhagavad Gita**, which tells of Krishna's instruction of his disciple Arjuna, is one of the fundamental holy scriptures of Hinduism.

In **The Ramayana**, we learn of the trials of Lord Rama, who was to have ascended to the throne but was banished to live for many years in the jungle with his lovely bride. Hanuman, the monkey deity, brings Lord Rama's captured bride a message from Rama and arranges her rescue.

The Ramayana, by any measure, is a literary masterpiece, vast in scope, long in stanzas and perfectly constructed poetry, accomplished in India in an era that may predate the poetic accomplishments of Homer in Greece. When translated in English, its poetic perfection remains. It's amazing what people could accomplish in the days before electricitiy, when they weren't so distracted by cell phones and television!

And speaking of ancient marvels, the Konark Sun Temple, about one thousand years old, was a wonder to behold. It was shaped rather like a pyramid, with many terraces and statues, including two great stone statues of elephants. We wandered around it, filming, greeting mischievous monkeys and studying the images carved into the stone.

AT THE ASHRAM OF SRI YUKTESWAR

Later, we drove again along the ocean road in Puri, beside the white sand beaches and pounding surf. Numerous Indian ladies in colorful, fluttering saris walked beside their husbands and children along the beach. It was mid-morning, and the heat was increasing. We heard on the radio that the previous day a temperature of 129 degrees Fahrenheit was recorded elsewhere in the same state of Orissa. It was horribly hot in Puri, also!

While we were in Puri, Paul was intent on fulfilling a very specific ambition. He recalled that in Yogananda's **Autobiography of a**

Yogi, a beautifully written book we had both found exceptionally inspiring, Yogananda recounts how he had undergone monastic training at an ashram in Puri – the ashram of his wise and devoted guru, Swami Sri Yukteswar. Yogananda's autobiography describes many things about his discipleship to Sri Yukteswar in Puri.

We had seen the image of Babaji earlier in our journey, a reminder of the param-guru of Swami Sri Yukteswar (his guru's guru). Paul hoped we could find the late Sri Yukteswar's ashram where Yogananda had studied, so we could visit it.

After a couple of inquiries, we arrived at a narrow street that we were told was near the ashram. Passing by some of the gentle, ubiquitous cows, we arrived at a place which looked like the compound of a private residence. Our driver led us to the entrance door of the walled compound. We rang a buzzer and were greeted by a cheerful, elderly gentleman in the robes of a Hindu monk.

It is amazing how open and welcoming people in India often prove to be to visitors who are total strangers. It is so very different than the United States, a nation where people tend to be on the defensive, always thinking first of the harm that could befall them if they greet a stranger.

When Indians intuitively detect that the stranger is sincere in his purpose and poses no imposition, doors open and then one receives a demonstration of the goodness and warmth of spirit which is prevalent among certain esteemed persons in India. Of course there are serious conflicts among people in India, too, and sometimes the people of different religions clash to the point of causing violence. Nevertheless, there is an over-riding phenomenon in India that the visitor is given the benefit of the doubt, and warmth and generosity often come quickly in a new relationship. It may have something to do with the "namaste" philosophy, the greeting that says, in effect, I honor the godliness or divinity that is within you.

The monk quickly understood our desire and was determined to assist us. He led us on a footpath through a pleasant garden into a modest building which is the sanctuary. We removed our shoes before entering. The building was fairly long with a raised platform at the far end. The only light was natural sunlight coming in from a few windows, which made a subdued, pleasant effect. Above the platform was a full-length painting of Sri Yukteswar.

Paul recalled for us a story from Yogananda's autobiography. It was at a time when the Rath Yatra ceremony was approaching, and Sri

An image of Swami Sri Yukteswar (center) with his disciple,
Paramahansa Yogananda (left)

Within this shrine are the remains of Swami Sri Yukteswar
at the Karar Ashram in Puri

Yukteswar ordered his devotees to walk barefoot along the beach to reach the point where they could attend the ceremonies and offer assistance.

Yogananda had recoiled at the thought of walking barefoot on what he knew would surely be blistering hot sand. Sri Yukteswar chastised him for his lack of faith, and Yukteswar promptly appealed to the Divine Mother to solve their problem.

Very soon afterwards, the bright, hot blue sky became overcast. Yogananda recalled that by the time they walked on the sand beach, it had cooled to the point where they did not need to worry about blisters.

Such was the faith of these Indian sages, who believed that the creator of the universe, present in every atom of creation, responds to the soul-calls of devotees who, as Krishna counseled, see the Lord present within all of his creation.

Was this degree of faith really so different from what Jesus taught? Wasn't it Jesus who said "Ask and ye shall receive"? Didn't he advise that those with faith could move mountains?

How much there is that unites the Christian and the Hindu, and how seldom we stop to realize it!

As we walked through the room with the painting of Sri Yukteswar and photos and artifacts that surely went back to the days of Yogananda, we all felt reverence. We also felt privileged to have been given the permission to be there. Our group bowed in respect, and we all sat on the floor. We all took the time to pray and meditate.

Perhaps twenty minutes later we were taken to the place of Sri Yukteswar's "mahasamadhi." This was the structure, a sort of shrine, where the great Indian guru's remains rest in peace.

In Hinduism, cremation after death is the rule. However, generally this does not apply to holy men, whose remains are kept intact. In Hinduism, the goal of the soul or spirit is to attain "samadhi," which means complete one-ness with God, the merging of the tiny individual ego into the vastness of creation and the Creator.

"Mahasamadhi" is the conscious exit of a yogi's soul from his earthly form at the moment of death. Sri Yukteswar passed while in meditation in a yoga posture, and there he remains behind a sealed wall in the structure we were permitted to visit.

Soon after leaving that shrine, Paul and Anil explained in detail to the caretaker about the nature of our project and where we were from. The caretaker told us that about two months earlier, Ricky Martin, the "La Vida Loca" singer from Puerto Rico, had also visited the ashram. Ricky Martin, it turns out, is a spiritual seeker.

We made a donation, and Paul bought a couple of rare books before we thanked the caretaker and left.

Paul was delighted that, in effect, we had paid homage to Babaji and Sri Yukteswar on the journey. He hoped that when we reached Kolkata (Calcutta), we could visit Yogananda's childhood home.

THE BATHING OF THE DEITIES

After a light lunch in an air-conditioned restaurant and some iced drinks, we set off again in our SUV. We asked our driver to take us to a large, open plaza in front of the Jagannath Temple.

Previously, we had made arrangements to pay a fee and be allowed to walk upstairs to the top of a building. Space was at a premium in that area that was swarming with pilgrims, and an overhead vantage point of the Rath Yatra ceremony was worth gold.

The area we had selected had a viewing platform with a large cloth canopy for shade and had a good view of the area. Nearby was a balcony (a bathing ghat) at the front of the temple on which there were large three-dimensional images of three Hindu deities that had been taken from the temple for this occasion: Lord Jagannath, his elder brother Balabhadra and sister Subhadra. "Daita" servitors – the Lords' bodyguards – bathed these representations of the deities with aromatic water and milk from one hundred eight sacred urns. Once again, there was that special number one-hundred eight that is shared by three major religions, the same as the number of rosary beads for Catholics and prayer beads for Buddhists.

Later, the Simhari servitors dressed the deities in ostentatious robes while thousands of devotees watched with hands folded in prayer. To the British Christians who colonized India a century ago, such practices might have been considered worship of idols, one of the reasons the British considered Hinduism a "heathen" religion. Our understanding of these practices today is much broader. The "deities" that are bathed in these ceremonies and then rolled on carts through the streets are symbols for aspects of the Godhead, the divine force behind our universe. Christians place values on symbols too, whether it be statues of Jesus and Mary, crucifixes that hang from rear view mirrors in cars or rosary beads. The fact that the symbols differ between religions does not seem a valid reason for people of one religion to reject the practices of another.

As the ceremony continued, one of our filming team members whispered to me that he was feeling nauseous and dizzy from the terrible heat and humidity. I was not feeling my best, either.

I told Paul that if I was not needed right then, I would head back to our air-conditioned hotel for a break. The other member and I squeezed our way through the massive crowd, found a yellow, three-wheeled scooter taxi and headed back.

More throngs of people were pouring into Puri from all directions. It was a swarming maze of human beings the likes of which I had never seen before in my life. The huge, wooden floats for transporting the deities in the next part of the Rath Yatra ceremony were being completed at the side of the street nearby.

If young Jesus was actually here, as the Shankaracharya had done his very best to confirm, I was certain Jesus would have witnessed the same ceremony, which has been repeated for over two thousand years.

Throngs of humanity come to Jagannath for the Rath Yatra Festival

6. A Journey to Kolkata (Calcutta)

*"A good traveler has no fixed plans
and is not intent upon arriving."*
---Lao Tzu

I awoke in the early morning light and smelled some kind of chemical fumes. Our train was entering the sprawling outskirts of Kolkata. I sat up in the train berth and rubbed my eyes. Through the years, I had heard a lot of stories about Kolkata (formerly known as Calcutta) – mind-boggling masses of people, vehicles, sacred cows, beggars, buildings, pollution, noise, and all the evils of urban life that come from intense over-crowding – New York to the tenth power. Well, I thought, we are about to see and experience it for ourselves!

Sanjay had decided that it would be convenient for us simply to stay in the upstairs "hotel rooms" at the Kolkata Central Train Station. What we gained in convenience of location we sacrificed in humane living conditions.

When we arrived, a group of porters helped us carry our baggage upstairs. Though most of our luggage had wheels and handles and could easily have been pulled across the ground, for some unknown reason, porters in India always carry luggage atop their heads. They reject the easy method and prefer the ancient one.

We entered a long, empty hallway with a smooth, hard, stone-type surface. We walked the length and near the end, we turned into a room on the left side. Our whole team would be staying in one very large dormitory-style room. Our porters put our baggage down, we paid them, they smiled and then left.

The room had a stone floor and barren walls. There were about fifteen or so cheap metal bunk beds and thin mattresses, with curious-looking metal brackets extending upwards (which, we learned later, are for holding mosquito netting). Those metal brackets all seemed to have sharp points and presented a constant challenge for us to avoid having our eyes poked out. One careless step near the beds and some-one would have lost an eye.

The far end of the room, away from the door, was mostly windows with metal bars, but no curtains or blinds, facing a nasty-looking melange of behind-building garbage dumps, weeds, and old electrical wiring. No paintings on the walls, no mirrors, no telephone, no television, but there was an adjoining bathroom. It had a tile floor, a sink and faucets, a hole-in-the-floor porcelain toilet, and a high, small window.

Arrival at Calcutta where manual labor is seen everywhere

Our whole team stood silently for several, long seconds, just looking around at everything in disbelief. I wish we had had a video camera on a tripod running. It would have been precious! This place was grim, even by Indian standards.

Finally, someone smiled and said, "Well gentlemen, we have arrived in the Black Hole of Calcutta!"

We were in hell and paying for that privilege in rupees.

We all roared with laughter for several seconds and then began to unpack our bags. Yes, the place did remind us of either a hospital room in a totally impoverished Third World country or a dingy prison. Fortunately, our stay in this particular lodging would be brief.

The Black Hole of Calcutta, incidentally, refers to an infamous incident during the India Rebellion of 1857, in which captured British soldiers were cast into a dark, circular holding pit which became known as the Black Hole of Calcutta.

Soon, we had all bathed, put on fresh clothes, gotten our equipment ready and walked downstairs. A quick check told us no one had

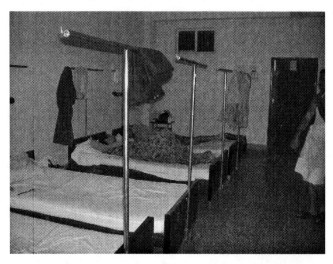

*Our lodging in Calcutta, where the beds had brackets for
mosquito nets that could have poked our eyes out*

punctured an eye on the mosquito net brackets.

At the ground level of the train station we found a fast food Indian restaurant which served our needs of the moment.

Paul was fascinated by the way the naan, or bread, was prepared there. It was in the shape of a large, puffy, upside-down ice cream cone, coming to a point at the top and hollow inside. He decided to take a picture of it to show back home.

His snapping of the flash picture practically set off an international incident or World War III.

One of the patrons having breakfast at a table nearby strenuously objected to the photo being taken and the possibility that his image might be in the picture. He began yelling and screaming about it in Hindi.

Paul became quite obsequious and apologetic, which didn't do much good since the objecting patron didn't understand him. Paul quickly tucked the camera away in his case, out of sight. At least for all that trouble, the picture did come out, though Anil was quite dark with no light on him in the background.

After breakfast there we all loaded into two yellow taxis and were on our way in search of the trail of Swami Abhedananda! He was the swami of great reputation who had lived for twenty-five years in the United States, and who, upon his return from India, had investigated

*Anil Urmil contemplates the naan bread in the shape of
an upside-down ice cream cone*

the question of the ancient manuscript Notovitch claimed to have
translated.

The swami was now deceased, but the question was, could we
find holy people in India of the Ramakrishna movement with whom
Swami Abhedananda would have been associated, who could further
enlighten us about the swami's findings on Notovitch? We weren't
quite sure where to go, but we had some ideas.

THE MAGNIFICENT HOWRAH BRIDGE

Nearby, within a distance of several hundred yards from the Calcutta Train Station, we could see the towering, silver-colored arches of
the Howrah Bridge. This bridge spans the Hoogly River, a branch of
the mighty Ganges, which forms a huge delta in West Bengal. The
Howrah Bridge is the third longest cantilever bridge in the world. A
magnificent sight!

As we drove across the bridge, we saw that it was teeming with vehicles and pedestrians. Some of the people on foot carried opened umbrellas to ward off the bright sunlight. It was already becoming hot,

A Taxi Traffic Jam in Kolkata and the Howrah Bridge

even in the morning.

We were headed for Ramakrishna Vedanta Math, the ashram of Swami Abhedananda. At this time, I will quote a passage from the dust cover of Abhedananda's book, **Journey into Kashmir and Tibet**:

Swami Abhedananda, the illustrious Apostle of Sri Ramakrishna Paramahansadev, visited London for the first time in the year 1896 at the clarion call of his brother-disciple Swami Vivekananda. After twenty-five years of spiritual ministration in England, America and many other European Countries, he returned to India in the year 1921 for serving his motherland till the end of his eventful life.

While in America the Swami came across the book **The Unknown Life of Jesus Christ** by the Russian traveler Nicolas Notovitch, which revealed the fact that Jesus Christ lived in India during the sixteen years of his unknown life, i.e., from 13 to 28 years of his age. Materials of the book were stated to have been collected by the writer from a manuscript on the life of Jesus Christ in the Hemis

Monastery in Ladakh where he happened to stay for some time for treatment by the Lamas.

In order to check up the truth, Swami Abhedananda immediately upon return to India started his journey to Tibet through Jojila Pass on the 14th July 1922, from Belur Math, when he was the Vice-President of the Ramakrishna Math and Ramakrishna Mission and returned to Belur Math on December 11, 1922, after a highly successful journey.

While in the Hemis Monastery Swami Abhedananda discovered an ancient manuscript in Tibetan language which unraveled the unknown chapter in the life-story of Jesus Christ. With the help of a local Lama interpreter he had the same translated in parts which have been included in Chapters 12 and 15 of this book *Journey into Kashmir and Tibet*.

Swami Abhedananda made it a rule to jot down in his diary the details of all that happened in the course of his journey in Kashmir and Tibet which he incorporated in his book, in Bengali, *Kashmir-O-Tibbate*, along with matters, both cultural and historical, relating to the countries like China, Japan, Korea, etc., while correcting and improving the manuscript for the book, of which this is the first published English Edition.

The account given by Swami Abhedananda about the unknown life of Jesus Christ in Chapters 12 and 15 corroborates the extracts from the book, *The Unknown Life of Jesus Christ* by N. Notovitch on the same aspects, given in Appendix one of this book. Appendix two gives the full text of the Hemis manuscript on *The Life of Saint Issa* by Nicolas Notovitch as translated from the French by Violet Crispe (1895).

(This ends the quotation from the dust cover of *Journey into Kashmir and Tibet* by Swami Abhedananda).

TO THE ASHRAM

The driver of our taxi thought he knew the location of Swami Abhedananda's ashram. It turned out that he dropped us off at a different ashram. The Hindu priests there were helpful and some of them spoke very good English. After some explanation, they understood where we wanted to go and pointed out directions, using a large map of Kolkata. It was our good fortune that a driver with an air-conditioned SUV showed up.

Anil negotiated with him and we soon had him as our driver for the rest of the day.

We drove on through what seemed to me like an endless labyrinth of streets and avenues, teeming with cars, buses, rickshaws, motorcycles, wandering sacred cows and stray dogs. I'm so glad I did not have to drive there!

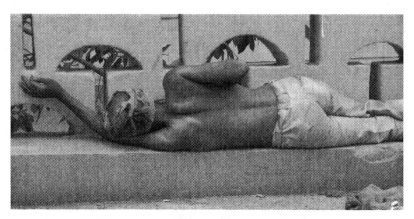

An exhausted laborer, lying at the side of a road in Calcutta

At last, we reached a relatively quiet side street and arrived in front of the ashram: Ramakrishna Vedanta Math. The address is: 19 A & B, Raja Rajkrishna Street, Kolkata - 700 006, India.

Binny rang the buzzer and we were greeted by a pleasant Hindu monk who ushered us all into a narrow courtyard between two buildings.

We removed our shoes and were also greeted by a friendly black and white cat. We followed the monk into a small office and met the director of the publications department.

We explained our project and also asked about a disciple of Swami Abhedananda's named Swami Prajnanananda. The director said that all those of the older generation had passed away. Only younger monks remained. However, he said we would be welcome to visit rooms where Abhedananda had lived and to see his possessions that were still kept there.

Once again, this was evidence of the extraordinary hospitality of Hindu monks in India. They did not know us, and we had no references. We had come in off the street. We had camera equipment, and they accepted our story without question.

We were allowed to film without anyone requiring a permit. They were gracious and went out of their way to answer all of our questions and show us everything they could about Swami Abhedananda. They wanted no money and in fact would not accept any when offered. They did say they would sell us copies of Abhedananda's books if we wished, and the prices of those books, well-produced in hard-back, were staggeringly small. I asked myself, could I imagine that kind of hospitality anywhere else but in India?

A GIFT FROM THOMAS EDISON

One of the ashram employees, Debasish Hore, led our group up-stairs to the rooms, which are maintained as when Abhedananda lived there. With the camera running, I made a mistake and said that the swami had lived in the west for twenty years. Debasish and the others heard and immediately corrected the mistake: "Twenty-five years!"

Ramakrishna Vedanta Math, where Swami Abhedananda,
lived and wrote many of his books in the 1920's

I thought to myself, look how quickly the devotees of Swami Abhedananda come to the defense of his personal history – they won't let me accidentally omit five years, turning them into "Missing Years" or "Hidden Years." So then how was it that the ancient Christians left eighteen years of the Lord of Lords out of the New Testament?

We entered the rooms and were shown the originals of many of Abhedananda's manuscripts and letters. Then we noticed that on the floor, tucked away beneath an old table, was a vintage phonograph from the earliest days of recordings. Debasish said that Swami Abhedananda was friends with Thomas Edison in America. Edison, they said, had become engrossed in long talks with the swami about Vedanta philosophy, the essence of Hinduism. After one such lengthy talk, Edison was so inspired that he gave Abhedananda the phonograph as a present.

And then one of the young monks began to play the ancient phonograph, to demonstrate it for us! There was an expression of such glee on his face, a smile a mile wide. What pride there was. The old record was scratched and one almost couldn't bear to listen to it, but for that monk, its existence, and the fact that it was a gift from the great Thomas Edison, was truly a miracle still.

As we continued making our way through the personal quarters of the late Swami Abhedananda, I suddenly came upon a treasure. On a wall high above a cabinet was a strikingly wonderful drawing of Jesus Christ. Jesus had the crown of thorns and his eyes were closed. There was a colossal serenity in the Lord's expression.

I asked about the drawing and was told it was one of the oldest known drawings of Jesus. Debasish told us that it had been a gift from Nicolas Notovitch to Swami Abhedananda. The monks knew nothing of its origins beyond that. We filmed it for **"Jesus in India."**

Before leaving we bought some additional copies of ***Journey into Kashmir and Tibet***, and Paul stocked up on a number of Abhedananda's other books on every imaginable subject, from psychology to the meaning of death to reincarnation. We thanked everyone and insisted upon leaving a donation.

It had already been a day to remember. But it was still hardly beginning. Back in our SUV, we decided to visit the location of the childhood home of Paramahansa Yogananda. We were told it is not open to the public, but at least we could see the outside and visit the neighborhood. And on the way there was another surprise, as we passed by the mission house of Mother Teresa!

VISIT TO THE MISSION OF MOTHER TERESA

Our driver, as always, remained with his vehicle to safeguard it as we entered the Mission of Mother Teresa. We walked inside through the open doors and to our shock we were met by a terrible stench of dozens of emaciated-looking, terribly sick people lying everywhere about. Catholic nuns were going to and fro, assisting those who were suffering. We spoke briefly with one nun, asking her if she had any opinion about whether Jesus had ever come to India. She smiled and said, "We are not scholars or researchers; we are simply nuns, helping the sick and dying. But I do not believe that Jesus was ever in India. How would he have come here? It is a long way from Palestine." Then she turned and walked away.

It was not a comment to which one wanted to reply.

Producer Anil Kumar Urmil pays respects to
a statue of Mother Teresa

I found this information in *India: DK Eyewitness Travel Guide* which I quote here:

"Mother Teresa (1910-1997), born Agnes Gonxa Bojaxhiu in Albania, came to Calcutta in 1929 to begin life as a teacher. The poverty and suffering she saw impelled her to leave the convent. She set up the order of the Missionaries of Charity, and her indefatigable work among the lepers, the terminally ill, the unwanted and the poor earned her universal respect and love. To the people of Kolkata she was just 'Mother,' and their love for her transcended boundaries of religion, class and community. She was awarded the Nobel Prize in 1979."

At the tomb of Mother Teresa in Kolkata (Calcutta)

THE BOYHOOD HOME OF YOGANANDA

We next drove to the childhood home of the author of *Autobiography of a Yogi*: Paramahansa Yogananda, the founder of Self-Realization Fellowship.

We parked our SUV under some nearby shade trees.

Paul and most of our team walked out to set up the tripod and do some filming. I walked around for a little while but I was suffering a lot from the terrible heat and humidity. Since I was not needed then for the filming, I quickly returned to the shade and the SUV. Our driver had the doors and windows of the SUV opened and was relaxing. I walked to a nearby stall and bought ice-cold Pepsis and popsicles for both of us. The driver was delighted and thanked me with a beaming smile.

It seemed that a long time went by. Madhu returned briefly with the news that while they were filming, an elderly man who lived nearby came out and invited Paul inside his home. It turned out that this family was related to Tulsi Bose, a childhood friend of Yogananda. They began to entertain Paul and the rest of our team by sharing a lot of old photographs and materials. I knew that all of this was important to Paul, so I just relaxed and tried to stay cool – literally. Everyone returned after a while and we all went to eat at an air-conditioned Indian restaurant.

Paul recounted for me what had taken place. Once again, it was a testament to the Indian spirit. These people had never met Paul, never heard of him, and yet upon hearing of his love of Yogananda, they opened their home to him to show him their shrine dedicated to Yogananda and the Self-Realization Fellowship gurus and saints. One room, painted all in dark blue, was filled with photos of the gurus, and they showed Paul the relic of a trident (a symbol of Shiva) that they claimed that Babaji had given to Yogananda, and which Yogananda had bequeathed to their family. They told stories of Yogananda's return visit to India after Yogananda spent over a decade in America. They remarked on how large Yogananda had become. They showed

A private family shrine to Yogananda and the SRF saints in Yogananda's neighborhood where he spent his youth in Kolkata (Calcutta)

Paul a bed that they said Yogananda had once slept in, which they said was really too small for him. They went on and on, including the story that never once had they eaten onions, because Yogananda had advised against it.

There was a great electricity to this encounter among strangers. It was as though they knew one another instantly. Indians might conjecture that they had known one another in a previous life!

How hot it was in Calcutta while the Film Crew was there!
Paul Davids (center) with relatives of Tulsi Bose

Around sunset we returned to our room at the Calcutta Train Station, freshened up and packed our baggage. We then got our porters, loaded everything into two yellow taxis and headed across the city and across the Howrah Bridge to the departure point for our express bus to Darjeeling ---- in the Himalayas!

Pedestrians cross the Howrah Bridge in Kolkata

7. Night Bus to Darjeeling

Lord Krishna once said that sometimes his enemies make
much more rapid spiritual progress than his devotees.
"How could that be?" asked a disciple.
"My enemies," said Krishna, "think of me constantly,
but my devotees only think of me when they want something."
---folklore from India

Madhu and I rode together in the same taxi with some of our group's baggage. The sun was setting and the air felt cooler as we sped along in the taxi.

"Forty cities in forty days," mused Madhu, as he gazed out the windows. "It's really quite astonishing – almost incredible," he remarked.

"Yes," I said, "Paul, Anil and I put together an amazingly ambitious filming schedule – I'd say that we strung together a daunting array of places."

"Yes, indeed!" he replied.

Madhu had a distinguished career with the Indian Navy and had traveled all over India. But now, even he was seeing some new places!

Our two taxis arrived at the boarding location for the express bus, which was beside a garden-like park. We unloaded our thirteen pieces of baggage (one large one had already been sent back to Goa from Orissa with one of our coordinators, Rajesh Parida).

Binny paid and tipped the taxi drivers, and we were soon loading our things onto the bus. There were no restrooms anywhere, and I noticed that various passengers were slipping into the bushes in the park. It was tempting.

Binny soon asked Paul and me if we wanted any dinner. We said that something light would be fine. He went to some nearby vendor stalls in the park and returned with a couple of cardboard boxes of chicken biryani and Lay's Potato Chips and two cold Pepsi Colas. Good ol' Binny! Always looking out for us.

It is a fact of life that Lay's Potato Chips and the Pepsi Cola company have their tentacles in every corner of life in India – and if not their tentacles, then one could say their billboards. Advertisements for Lay's and Pepsi are simply everywhere, seemingly more than any other products. Wake up, Coca-Cola, Pepsi seems to be the drink that won the hearts and minds of the people of India. One wonders if those companies constituted a silent American invasion as long ago as when the British took over the country, and then they simply never withdrew when the era of colonialization ended. I say that tongue-in-cheek, of course, but it's a marvel how one can be in the most out of the way places, climbing up bluffs in the jungle surrounded by dense vegetation and palm trees, and there in the middle of the wilds one can almost bank on seeing a Pepsi and Lay's Potato Chip ad, sometimes painted onto a crumbling wall of an old hut!

A GRUMPY BUS DRIVER

Not long after dark, a heavyset Indian man with an unpleasant disposition arrived – our bus driver. He and his assistant each carried a small overnight bag. The driver, with an unsmiling face, stood up and recited the bus rules in Hindi and briefly in English, and then we took off. I was glad to be underway and thinking ahead about cooler weather, high up in the mountains! I was also glad I had taken a visit to the bushes when I couldn't find a bathroom. The rules of the road on this bus did not include mercy stops for passengers in dire need of relieving themselves. Control your bladder (and more) or die of embarrassment, that seemed to be the rule on certain lengthy bus trips. There was no passenger bill of rights – especially not with the fellow who was driving us up into the mountains.

Paul was sitting nearby at a window seat, and I saw that he soon leaned back and dozed off. It had been a long, hard day in the terrible heat. The air conditioning on the bus helped me to imagine that we were already in the cool mountains.

I leaned back in my seat also and enjoyed gazing out the windows at the passing parks and lighted buildings.

Eventually – very eventually –our bus stopped at a way-station sort of bus stop. There were several vendors' stalls selling Pepsi Colas and Lay's Potato Chips, hot tea, biscuits (various kinds of wafer-type cookies) and other snacks. People could walk to an alleyway or bushy area to relieve themselves, because there were no bathrooms at these side-of-the-road sorts of stops.

Some people took the chance to smoke cigarettes; some of the Indian men made a fist, holding the cigarette between the middle and ring fingers. Then, with the fist as a kind of chillum, they inhaled from the thumb and index finger area. I have tried it myself, and I know why they do it. The rumors are true. It does give you a buzz!

At the end of the break, our driver yelled in a grouchy kind of way, and everyone got quickly back on the bus, lest they be left behind.

As our journey progressed through the night, we traveled northward into more rural and open areas. Most of the passengers tried to lean back in their seats and get some sleep. Once, in the wee hours, our bus hit a bad bump and many of us woke up.

Several of our team members felt the need for a restroom break. We asked Binny to talk to the driver. There was a heated exchange in Hindi and then after they almost came to blows – truly, Binny was ready to slug the driver – our bus finally stopped at the side of the road. We were quick about it and soon continued on our way. The bus driver scowled at us whenever we made eye contact for the rest of the journey, as if to rub it in that it had been our fault that he lost five minutes on the way up the mountain, and that we should have controlled our bodily functions for a few more hours without inconveniencing him.

I woke up just before the sun came above the horizon and was delighted to see tea plantations. We were speeding through a gently rolling landscape with a vast number of tea bushes in all directions, heading for Darjeeling. There were quite a few scattered trees, and to the north, forested mountains.

We eventually (very eventually) took a rest stop at a roadside tea stall. I think it was the first time that I was ever drinking tea while at the same time I was able to touch living tea plants!

PIT STOP AT SILIGURI

Our bus trip came to an end at a town called Siliguri, which lies a long way down the mountainside to the south of Darjeeling. Our driver, who had not gotten any more cheerful during our journey, dropped us off at the edge of Siliguri. His assistant helped us unload our baggage – all thirteen pieces (a lucky number for me) – onto the dirt roadside, away from the pavement. The bus then sped off, kicking up some dust as a final insult.

The next part of our journey to Darjeeling would be in an SUV. Binny, Anil, and Madhu sauntered off to waylay a driver and make a deal.

Paul and I were groggy from sleep deprivation and about to wilt in the heat. We took refuge in the shade of a tree beside a roadside vendor. We sat on plastic chairs in the dirt and each nursed a cup of tea.

Even early in the morning, the weather was still oppressively hot and humid. We had not gotten into the cool mountain elevation yet.

Flies buzzed around, and emaciated garbage dogs wandered by as passing vehicles sent drifting dust. I winced and glanced sideways at Paul, feeling embarrassed that we were seeing such a gritty side of India. Then I noticed an old playing card lying in the gutter. I picked it up and handed it to Paul. He smiled and immediately did a sleight-of-hand disappearing card trick. If he was irritated by the tough journey, he didn't show it at all. As always, he was a real trooper!

At a nearby place called Bagdogra, there was an airstrip. Also close by was the famous "toy train," which makes the journey up the mountainsides to Darjeeling. We had discussed taking the train, but Sanjay had cautioned us that the train was rather slow, and he thought that perhaps our abundance of baggage could also be an issue. Thus, we planned to set out and continue all the way from Siliguri in the SUV.

After a long half an hour, a gleaming white SUV pulled up and our team members smiled and said: "Get in!"

They had found a young man worthy to drive us, and they had made a deal. We gratefully climbed in and buckled up. Oh, what a joy to have air conditioning! Never again, I told myself, would I take it for granted.

Binny, in the front seat, grinned and handed back two plastic bottles of ice-cold water. Another joy!

Soon we were barreling along the two-lane paved road through more and more tea plantations. Our driver was playing the radio; the Indian music had a lovely female voice accompanied by sitar and tabla. Within an hour we had begun to reach densely forested mountains. Then we were able to turn off the air conditioning and roll down the windows.

Cool air rolled in with the fragrance of the forest.

At last!

Before long, we heard a shrill train whistle, and to one side of the road, we saw the "toy train." The blue-colored train cars were moving slowly, negotiating sharp turns on the mountainside. The engineer and passengers gave us a cheerful wave. We waved and continued upward,

High in the Himalayan mountains in the mists of Darjeeling

speeding along and passing the train. I noticed the name "Chomol-ungma" painted in big white letters on the side of the leading train car, and I remembered it as a Tibetan name for Mount Everest, meaning "Goddess Mother of the World." A good omen!

TO THE PLACE OF THE THUNDERBOLT!

We continued driving upwards in the SUV along countless switchbacks. The two lane paved road was narrow, and at times we slowed down when a bulky truck met us. The vegetation was always lush on the mountainsides; not dense conifer forests, but vines, bushes and various trees. The sky became overcast as we climbed, and the air coming in the windows was cooler. At times, there was a cool, drifting fog and sometimes even a few raindrops fell.

Our destination for that day was Darjeeling, which in the Tibetan language means "dorje" (thunderbolt) and "ling"(place).

From several locations in the Darjeeling area it is possible – weather permitting – to see Mount Kanchenjunga (Mount of Five Treasures), the third highest mountain in the world. Although we intended to film in Darjeeling (and one of the best interviews I gave was done over cups of hot tea in a cozy restaurant with rain tapping at the windows), our visit to Darjeeling had no direct connection to our research about Jesus in India. However, there were several indirect connections.

One of those was that the distinguished Russian explorer and artist, Nicholas Roerich, had visited Darjeeling in the 1930's. He painted some beautiful paintings of Mt. Kanchenjunga (see www.roerich.org and click on"prints"and then "Kanchenjunga"). Another of my favorites is "Milarepa." One may also click on "the collection" and "paintings" to access more. Roerich was also one of the witnesses to the *Life of St. Issa* document at Hemis Monastery in Ladakh in 1926.

Also, there is a significant Tibetan community living at and near Darjeeling. Personally, I have always liked and admired the Tibetan people. When I was in the Peace Corps in Afghanistan, I had read Heinrich Harrer's classic book, *Seven Years in Tibet*, and also Michael Peissel's *Cavaliers of Kham*.

Various traditions and legends hint that some Tibetans may have secret knowledge about Jesus having visited Tibet 2,000 years ago. This would have been after Jesus fled Jagannath to avoid assassination. There has always been an inexplicable mystery over the fact that Tibetan Buddhists use precisely 108 prayer beads, and the Catholic Rosary also uses 108 beads. Hindus also revere the number 108. No one should suppose that's a coincidence.

We hoped to talk with some scholarly Tibetans and see if they knew anything about this.

About halfway up the mountain, we stopped at a tea shop and stretched our legs. The cloud cover had parted and bright sun shone on us for a while. The temperature was significantly cooler than in the sweltering lowlands.

Looking through the open windows toward the back of the tea house, we could see a large, ball-like water tank. It appeared to be about five feet in diameter, made of black plastic, and apparently it was used to collect rainwater. We later saw many of those in that region.

Late in the afternoon, in the midst of a cool fog, we finally arrived in Darjeeling. The look and feel of the cool fog reminded me of the time, years ago, when I had arrived on foot at the remote village of Namche Bazaar. At that time, I was on a twenty-one day trek in Nepal to the base camp of Mount Everest. Darjeeling, by comparison, is a respectable city. Still, the feeling I had in the cool, Himalayan air was the same.

We drove directly to Hotel Chanakya, situated on the downhill side of Robertson Road in Darjeeling. Some hotel porters helped us carry our baggage up the narrow stairway to the second floor. Our rooms were very small and the bathrooms were tiny! No toilet paper and no towels. Well, I thought , we won't be staying here very long!

MOUNTAIN OF FIVE TREASURES

We all did a little unpacking, freshened up, and then Paul, Binny, and I decided to go for a little walk. We had asked at the front desk about viewing locations for possibly seeing Mount Kanchenjunga. They told us that about 300 to 400 meters away was a viewing place. The pathway was all paved and it was safe in a forest. We carried our big video camera, the tripod and camera bag. We arrived after a short, pleasant walk. Along the way we met a steady flow of local walkers, many of them Tibetans. All were cheerful and some asked about our filming. Kanchenjunga, incidentally, is called "Mount of Five Treasures" because there are five peaks clustered fairly close together; the summit of Kanchenjunga being one of the five.

Looking downward, over the guardrail from our perch, we could see green slopes descending for thousands of feet. There was a covered bench beside us where we relaxed.

The fog never lifted that time.

The author arrives in Darjeeling in the fog

The next morning we tried again early, before sunrise. It was less foggy, but still mostly cloudy. Looking in the direction where we had been told, we saw that Kanchenjunga was still covered by clouds. Some locals told us that in the autumn, particularly November, the skies are often crystal clear and the views of Kanchenjunga can be great.

AN INTERVIEW AT RUMTEK

About mid-morning Paul, Binny, and I picked up our things and walked back in the direction of our hotel. Along the way we found a peaceful, Tibetan restaurant where the manager allowed us to do filming in a quiet room. This room had large windows and the view of the valley below was spectacular. Paul set up the tripod and filmed a lengthy interview with me that seemed to cover my whole life story. I recounted how I sold my house in Texas to have enough money to get my first book printed, and how I was ostracized by nearly everyone in Lampasas, Texas, for doing it. I quoted Krishnamurti, the Vedanta philosopher, who cautioned that whenever a person sets out to find the real truth about something, he had better be armed with great courage, because "he may not find what he is expecting to find." That, in essence, has been the story of my life. Courage has always come to me, but sometimes it takes a while to muster it.

The steaming cups of tea served to us during that interview still warm me even now as I write these words months later. High on that mountain, the little cubby-hole of a Tibetan restaurant was as cozy as anything I have experienced. But then the drizzle on the windowpanes turned to a torrent. The rain was beating hard, surrounding us. And at that point, needless to say, Paul turned off the microphone and the interview was over.

Afterwards, we returned to our hotel and learned from Madhu that some Tibetans had recommended that we visit the Rumtek Tibetan Buddhist Monastery. It is located a day's drive away, to the north, near Gangtok, in the Principality of Sikkim.

We all had a good lunch and then most of us took naps to recuperate some from the effects of the high altitude. I later went strolling around some local stores and found a good photography shop called Das Studio.

Late in the afternoon the clouds finally began to clear. I went back to the hotel and found Paul and Binny getting the camera gear ready for one more try at filming Kanchenjunga.

We all walked briskly back to the observation site.

To our great good fortune, just as we arrived, the clouds on the horizon parted and we had a clear view of the summit!

We stayed there quite a while and soaked in the incredible view. Paul must have filmed a half hour of footage, zooming in tight and then retreating from the mountain. The clouds seemed to dance across the sky, and shafts of light poured down as if sent from heaven. It was one of those rare epiphanies, an experience that elevates the mind and soul and lives on long after it is over.

The finale of **"Jesus in India"** shows me at the overlook that day, as I cited an Indian poem I had learned by heart long ago. It's called **Salutation to the Dawn** by Kalidasa. It goes like this.

"Look therefore to this day, for it is life, the very life of life. In its brief course lie all the verities and realities of your existence – the bliss of learning, the glory of action, the joy of knowledge. For yesterday is only a dream, and tomorrow is only a vision, but today well lived makes every yesterday a vision of happiness and every tomorrow a dream of hope. Look therefore to this day."

Later, we walked back to our hotel. We left early the next morning with our driver in his SUV, bound for Sikkim!

The Shops of Darjeeling

8. To the Kingdom of Sikkim

Long ago, in ancient India, there lived a Hindu holy man named Narada. He was an ascetic who spent years alone in a cave in the Himalayas, in deep meditation. At last, one day, Lord Shiva materialized before him and spoke: "Narada, as a reward for your devotion I have come to grant you a boon, a gift. Do you want anything?"

"Yes, indeed," replied Narada, "I want you to explain the mystery of the samsara, the maya, or illusion by which the earth plane seems so real."

Shiva sighed deeply and said, "Are you sure you want to ask that one? It never turns out very well."

"I insist!" replied Narada.

"Very well, but to give the answer, we must walk far, to a place in the desert" said Shiva. When they finally arrived among the sand dunes, Shiva spread a blanket in the shade of a small, solitary thorn tree. He then handed a drinking glass to Narada, saying, "Before I answer your question, bring me a drink of water. If you walk over that dune, you will find water."

Narada set off across the dune, and to his surprise, found a river on the other side. Just across the river he saw a well plowed field and a farm house. Deciding to get clean well water for Lord Shiva, he went to the house to ask permission. When he knocked at the door, the most beautiful maiden he had ever seen opened the door. "Won't you stay for dinner with my father and me?" she asked.

Narada said "Yes."

He was invited to help a few days with the harvest. He and the farmer's daughter fell in love, later married and had three lovely children. His father-in-law died and Narada became owner of the farm. He worked hard, was prosperous and had never been so happy in his life. In the 12th year, a terrible flood came and Narada, his wife, and three children had to flee, crossing the river. All perished, except for Narada, who was able to reach shore. He wept, totally devastated, lying in the sand.

The sun came out, Narada looked up and saw the drinking glass which Lord Shiva had given him long ago. It was full of rain water. He picked it up and walked across a nearby sand dune. To his amazement, nearby under a lone thorn tree, sat Lord Shiva!

Narada rushed over to him. Bending down, and wiping tears from his eyes, he handed the glass to Lord Shiva. Shiva opened his eyes from meditation and looked into Narada's face with deep compassion. "Narada, what took you so long?" said Shiva. "You've been gone almost half an hour."

---folk story from ancient India

I learned a long time ago, while in the Peace Corps in Afghanistan, that if four people and their luggage can fit comfortably into a vehicle, instead there will be six or seven people, not four. So it was with us, that our five filming team members plus our driver – and thirteen pieces of luggage – in one SUV, was crowded enough to make us all utterly miserable! Oh well, it would have been delightful in two vehicles, but our production budget was growing thin and we decided to economize!

The weather was mostly cloudy and a little foggy as we left Darjeeling. The two-lane paved road was, it seemed, always winding around switchback turns, either going down a mountainside or up one.

Sometimes we were following a slow-moving cargo truck for miles, while it belched diesel fumes. On one occasion, for a few miles the road paralleled a river which had a churning flow of muddy water.

We stopped at a tea house along the river. Paul and I had cold drinks (care to guess what brand?) and our Indian members had hot tea and potato chips (another mystery as to what type?) There was an extra bag of chips which Binny tossed our way.

The weather right then was mostly sunny and pretty warm. I relaxed with my cold Pepsi under a ceiling fan and talked with Binny about his family back in Bombay. Binny was a family man, and due to our filming, he had not seen his family in quite awhile. He was happily married and proud of his young son. Above all, religion held the life of his family together. He was not a Hindu, like Madhu, Sanjay and DM. He was a Christian – a **Thomas** Christian. He traced the roots of his branch of Christianity back to Apostle Thomas' preaching in India. Furthermore, he was devout. In his branch of Christianity, one prayed numerous times every day, beginning at the crack of dawn, at the first moments of waking consciousness. Whenever I had shared a room with him on this journey, or Paul had shared a room with him, we had awakened to the daybreak murmurs of Binny swiftly reciting his prayers.

This made for a most interesting contrast, in a way. I was the fallen-away fundamentalist Christian, raising questions in my writings and in the documentary film that challenged bedrock certainties that all faithful Christians by nature and training and inculcation did not question. Binny of course had no difficulty at all with the concept that Jesus had traveled to India in his youth. It presented no problem to him to consider that Jesus may have studied with and learned certain things from both Hindus and Buddhists. What did seem quite unthinkable to him was the possibility that Jesus had survived the crucifixion.

Hearing our talk, and knowing of our plans to visit the tomb of Yuz Asaf in Kashmir had aroused his curiosity. He wanted to go there.

He wanted to see it. But without any investigation or study of the evidence, he insisted that he knew that that was not Jesus in the Prophet's Tomb, the tomb of Yuz Asaf. For Binny, the resurrection and ascension of Jesus to heaven were facts as certain as the fact that the sun would rise in the morning, and that the flowers bloom in the spring.

This made for robust discussion, throughout the many weeks of our trip. I tried to get to the core reasoning behind his belief. It was not just because of what it said in the Bible. It was not because of what he had been taught as a youngster. For Binny, the proof of the reality of Christ's resurrection was the behavior of the Apostles after the crucifixion. The Apostles were certain they saw Jesus, they talked with him again, breathed beside him again in the same places, walked with him, ate with him, learned of their mission from him. For Binny, it was not conceivable that the Jesus the Apostles saw then, who astonished them and re-shaped their lives and gave them a faith that was invincible unto death – it was not conceivable that it was a Jesus who had come close to death and narrowly escaped being executed. For surely, said Binny, a Christ like that would have been a wounded, suffering, broken man with a broken body, a man requiring months of recovery before he could begin to walk again. That would not have been a man who could appear before them and instill them with an unbreakable belief in the Father and in themselves. Or that, as Saint Thomas said to Jesus after seeing the wounds, that Jesus was "my Lord and my God."

I respected Binny's beliefs deeply, but for me, the discussion did not end there at all, because if so, I would have had no argument and no interest in the tomb of Yuz Asaf in Kashmir. In the Bible it is clear that Jesus was only on the cross a matter of hours, and that his legs were not broken. It is clear he was taken down by nightfall. It is clear that his ally, Joseph of Arimathea, who owned the "rich man's tomb" where Jesus was taken, went to Pilate swiftly to plead for Jesus' body. It is clear that he told Pilate that Jesus had already expired, and that Pilate was surprised and hardly believed it at first but did give his assent to Joesph of Arimathea to take the "deceased" Jesus. Nicodemus, another ally of Jesus, and Joseph of Arimathea had the "body" in their possession, and a massive amount of alloes with remarkable antibiotic and healing properties were brought to anoint the body.

In Judaism, that is not the way of a corpse is anointed. It is a means of attempting to save a life. In Islam, there is a healing ointment that is called in Arabic "The Ointment of Issa." It refers to the healing herbs that were used on the Saviour after the crucifixion. There are ancient tombs in the region with more than one entrance. The mystery of the missing body, for me, is not the mystery as presented in the New Testament. Two "angels" were seen at the tomb with the rock in front of it rolled away. They asked the two Mary's: "Why do you seek the living among the dead? Your Lord is not here."

Thus, without letting faith capture and rule my thinking and interpretations, to me, the concept that Jesus survived, spoke to the Apostles afterwards and then traveled with his mother to Kashmir after undergoing a period of healing in Damascus is plausible. The possibility that Mary is buried in Murree, Pakistan, and that Jesus is buried as Yuz Asaf in the Rozabal tomb that is revered by Ahmadiyyan Muslims in Kashmir as the actual grave of Jesus, seems to me to be within the realm of the possible. It is certainly within the realm of the thinkable.

"No," insisted Binny. "The Apostles all suffered horrible deaths, sacrificing themselves for what they knew to be true: that Jesus was God and that he was resurrected from the dead. That is why they accepted the persecution and horrible fates they suffered."

Later, Prof. Alan Mitchell of Georgetown's Department of Divinity, a former Jesuit, would indicate in an interview for Paul that the fates of the Apostles was not so absolutely certain, historically, as Binny believed and assumed. That is another disputed point among scholars.

The fact that Binny and I were at loggerheads, regarding the inquiry and investigation, made for many interesting conversations, but it never for a moment interfered with our extraordinary working relationship. And Binny's doubts about the theory we were investigating never for a moment made him re-consider his devotion to working with us to complete the film.

And so, among our group, there was much more at work between us behind the scenes than was visible on the surface.

At any rate, we had arrived by SUV at an ancient cave that was a temple for Hindus, a temple of Shiva said to date back over five thousand years. We proceeded to that sacred cave to do some filming.

Soon, we were continuing on our way and stopped to film at a particularly beautiful place along the river. As we set up the camera tripod, some wild monkeys approached us. They were eager to explore our equipment and very curious.

We gave them some potato chips and cookie pieces. Wild monkeys are a common sight in India and Sikkim, especially along roadsides and near human dwellings. The reverence for Hanuman, the monkey deity, is a significant part of Hindu life. And of course, the Buddhists tend to respect and tolerate all forms of life, especially the mischievous and curious creatures, like monkeys.

Late in the afternoon, under an overcast sky, we arrived at Gangtok, the capital of Sikkim. Sikkim was formerly an independent country – a kingdom – but is now considered a part of India. Still, there are customs houses at the borders, and non-Indians must present passports to enter or leave Sikkim.

As we arrived at the Hotel Basar Residency on Tibet Road, my favorite umbrella went missing. Someone must have snatched it while we were unloading. I should have been a little more watchful. Well, I could buy another umbrella.

A rainy day in Sikkim

AT RUMTEK MONASTERY

After getting situated in our rooms, we got directions from the front desk staff and soon headed out again in the SUV. We were on our way to the Rumtek Tibetan Buddhist Monastery, situated a few miles away from Gangtok, on a forested mountainside. Light rain began falling as we drove out of Gangtok.

Several miles out of the city, we crossed a bridge over a river of white rapids. A sign at the far end of the bridge said in English: "Welcome to Rumtek Monastery."

We drove further up the paved road through a forest of beautiful, tall conifer trees. Higher up the mountainside we reached the monastery itself, a majestic complex of Tibetan-style buildings with sloped walls.

Several young monks, including some small boys, were wearing the traditional maroon and yellow Buddhist robes. They were playing a game of cricket in a grassy area near the buildings.

We left the SUV with the driver keeping watch, as always. As we approached the entrance of the main building, a white-haired monk greeted us with a smile and "namaste." He ushered us into the building and up a stairway. He led us to a spacious office and requested we sit down. Soon, two young monks entered with trays of tea cups and pots of hot tea. They also brought some cookies.

A middle-aged monk appeared, speaking excellent English. We explained the nature of our filming project and what we would like to discuss. He gave permission and asked us to set up our tripod and video camera. We then had a good interview, but practically no new information came up. He had heard legends and rumors, especially about secret information about Jesus or St. Issa at the Hemis Monastery in Ladakh. But he had no first-hand knowledge. He did, however, speculate that the Dalai Lama might be a source for the answer on this mystery. He also reminded us of how many libraries in Tibet were destroyed during conflict between the Tibetans and the Chinese, who caused the Dalai Lama to have to flee as a young man, when they declared Tibet to be part of China. It would be a sad conclusion to our search if it turned out that the original *Life of St. Issa* document in the Pali language, thought to have been at the Marbour Monastery in Tibet, had fallen victim to the massive destruction wrought by the armies and military conflict.

When we arrived back at the Hotel Basar Residency, Anil became ill with a badly upset stomach and a lot of nausea. We called a local doctor who came up to his room and examined him in bed. The doctor prescribed some medicine and said he should rest in bed a couple of days.

Madhu our production manager (striped shirt) amid soldiers and monks at the entrance to the Rumtek Buddhist Monastery

The combination of exotic food and high elevation was bothering all of us to some extent. The almost constantly cloudy weather and cold, drizzling rain recently had been depressing, also.

TO THE RAILHEAD AT NEW JALPAI GURI

After Anil recovered, we loaded up our things one morning and headed southward. We were bound for a place southwest of Sikkim called New Jalpai Guri. It is the railhead, or terminus point, for one part of the Indian railway system. At New Jalpai Guri we could board a train for the next part of our journey: to Benares (Varanasi) on the holy Ganges River. I had visited Benares before, on my first trip to India, when I had been serving in the Peace Corps in Afghanistan. I was looking forward to returning.

Hours later, after a long drive, we reached New Jalpai Guri. We were now in northeastern India, back in the hot, humid farmlands. Sanjay, always available by cell phone, had already booked our train tickets. However, because an unusual number of Indian government employees were traveling on that train, we could not get anything with air conditioning. So we had no choice but to reluctantly accept the situation.

Departing from Sikkim

9. Arrival at Varanasi

"You may enter Paradise," said the gatekeeper of Nirvana,
"but no dogs are allowed here, so you must leave your dog behind."
"This dog has saved my life several times," said Arjuna.
"If he cannot enter Paradise, then neither shall I."
At this, the dog transformed into the powerful image of
Shiva, saying: "You have passed a difficult test. Let us
both enter!"

---Hindu folk story

Our team boarded the express train for Varanasi just before five p.m. that day at New Jalpai Guri. Paul and I had seats close to each other in the middle part of the train. The rest of our team were sitting farther back, in one of the rear cars.

As always, Binny made contact just before the train started moving, bringing Paul and me each an ice-cold plastic bottle of drinking water.

He smiled, saying: "I'll check on you from time to time."

He turned and walked down the passageway. All the windows were open, and with no air conditioning, the temperature was about 105 degrees Fahrenheit, in the shade – and it was humid.

"Well, Paul," I said, "people in hell don't have ice water. So by comparison, we are lucky!"

Paul smiled a little as he wiped his brow with a handkerchief. We knew we were in for a hot, miserable evening, and that we would be hot until we arrived in Varanasi the next morning. Then, thankfully, our hotel would have air conditioning. It seemed a long way off.

I glanced around us at the other nearby passengers, all Indian citizens. They were of all ages and moderately well-off, because they could afford to be traveling a long distance on a train. None of them appeared to be particularly distressed about the heat and humidity.

We were all in the shade, and the train had begun moving. Some people were fanning themselves serenely. Paul was looking grim, and I wasn't feeling very rosy either. I tried in vain to remember some jokes.

As if reading my mind, one of the mature Indian men sitting across from us smiled and said: "Don't feel too bad – the sun will soon set, and the night air will be much cooler, especially since the train is moving. And you know, it was all those bloody government bureaucrats who pinched our air conditioning!"

Paul and I had a good laugh at that. I then took out my magic deck of shaved playing cards and handed them to Paul.

"Why don't you do some magic?" I asked.

Paul grinned and soon had us all enthralled.

AN INCREDIBLE PEPTO-BISMOL COMMERCIAL

Later that evening, Binny brought us a couple of hot box lunches and cold bottles of Pepsi with straws. I had been trying to think about all the bitterly cold winters I had spent in the interior of Alaska.

I remembered one entire month of January when the warmest temperature – day or night – was minus 28 degrees below zero Fahrenheit. And often at night it was minus 50 degrees, or minus 70 degrees – or colder! One memorable night, I was at a town near Fairbanks called North Pole when it was minus 83 degrees below zero Fahrenheit! And that was the actual temperature -- not wind chill -- because the air was dead still.

Perhaps I felt a little more thankful for the heat.

I was tired around bedtime and walked to the toilet.

I had to wait, so I took a seat near the passageway. Across from me sat an Indian family, traditionally dressed. The father wore a turban and white pajamas; the mother wore a colorful sari, and they had four teenage children. All of them were listening to some lively, Indian music on the radio. And everyone was drinking a bottle of Pepto-Bismol as they swayed and bounced to the music!

My mouth went open at the delightful strangeness of the sight! I glanced around, thinking that maybe someone was filming some kind of kinky Pepto-Bismol commercial.

No.

As the weirdness continued, I cautiously leaned toward them and saw that actually all of the pink bottles were of Strawberry-Flavored Nestle Milk! I laughed out loud, and they all bobbed their heads from side to side and cast looks at each other.

The toilet became unoccupied, and I left my seat.

Opportunity strikes.

Thank the Lord for small pleasures.

ON THE HOLY GANGES RIVER

We arrived in Varanasi (but I still like to call it Benares), and mercifully, there was a thick cover of clouds. That kept the searing temperatures down somewhat.

We went in two yellow taxis to The Gautam Hotel in the Ramkatora district of Varanasi. As always, Sanjay had pre-arranged our hotel stay. We checked in, cleaned ourselves up somewhat and got ready for filming.

As we arranged ourselves, a familiar banter of questions went around: "Are the batteries charging?" "How many are charged now?" "Who has the tripod?" "Should we bring the umbrellas?" "Where is the white balance paper?" "How is the light now?"

As Paul said sometimes: "We have become a real production team!"

From the holy Ganges River, a view of the boats by the shore

Soon, we re-boarded the taxis and were at the series of stone steps that lead down to the Ganges River itself. Hindus call the steps that descend to a river "ghats," and if the steps lead down to a swimming area (where people not only swim but also bathe or wash their clothes in the water), then they are called "bathing ghats." There are

lots of picturesque ghats in Varanasi, where people gather and social-
ize.

Standing on the ghats, it looked as wide and majestic as I had remembered from my first trip, so many years before. The lighting effect
of the overcast sky was surreal, soft and pastel and bordering on misty
white, as if to emphasize the Hindu belief that all is "maya," that what
we think is reality is only an illusion. It was like an experience out of a
dream.

We arranged a lengthy boat ride with a boatman and guide to
come with us. When we were all aboard, Paul set up the camera, and
we all set off.

The bathing ghats, with their quite massive stone steps, are on the
north side of the Ganges and extend along the river for many hundreds of meters. We videotaped the scenes of large masses of devout
Hindu pilgrims on the ghats. At the south banks of the river there is a
broad expanse of small stones. Toward the far eastern end of the ghats
is the place of human cremation.

No one is ever allowed to film there. We were cautioned by the
guide not to even consider it. That is considered an insult to the families of the deceased. However, one could observe that there were dead
bodies of all sizes; all were wrapped in cloth and some in bright-
colored cloth. There was smoke in the air from the burning of the
bodies. Amidst the morbidity of the cremations, not very far away
people bathed, washed their clothes in the Ganges and carried on as if
nothing unusual was occurring. And for the natives of Varanasi, this
was not unusual, it was a daily routine.

People came there from all over India for the express purpose of
dying. In their theology, those who die in the holy city of Varanasi and
are cremated on the banks of the holy river shall escape the karmic
cycle of birth and death and attain liberation. After all, the goal of attaining nirvana in Hinduism has escape from corporeal reality and the
sentient life as one of its attributes – to attain the bliss of departing
this world in a way such that one will never have to be re-born, never
experience life again.

We asked the boatman to turn us back westward, again paralleling
the bathing ghats. Our guide, a local Hindu man perhaps in his thirties,
spoke excellent English.

He told a lot of fascinating stories about the Ganges. We asked
him about pollution. There are many reports of pollution in the
Ganges. And although most deceased people are consigned to being

ashes before they are scattered in the river, in some cases bodies are placed directly in the river upon death. That includes babies. It also includes those who die from snake bites. We questioned the wisdom of bathing there and the whole concept of the river being holy. In the middle part of the river our guide scooped his hands into the water and drank directly from the river.

"It is like my mother," he said, "it will not harm me."

THE GREAT SAINT LAHIRI MAHASAYA

For some reason, Paul and I began talking about Paramahansa Yogananda and his teachings. Paul mentioned the fact that we had paid homage to Yogananda by visiting the neighborhood where he grew up in Calcutta, and we had visited the Karar Ashram of Yogananda's guru, Swami Sri Yukteswar.

"Sri Yukteswar's guru was the guru of Yogananda's parents," Paul said. "His name was Lahiri Mahasaya. I wonder where in India he lived?"

"Really, sir?" said our guide, in a tone of astonishment. "You do not know where is the home of Lahiri Mahasaya?"

"No, do you know?" Paul asked.

"Of course. Look up at the yellow house up there, with the flag." He pointed to a house we could clearly see up on the hill above the ghats. "Home of Lahiri Mahasaya!" he exclaimed.

Paul and I were surprised and stared at each other, both baffled and amazed. We had wondered where in all of India that Lahiri Mahasaya had lived, and it so happened that our boat on the Ganges was very close by, within sight of his house. How could that be? How can such coincidences exist?

"Lahiri Mahasaya was the guru of Sri Yukteswar who was the guru of Paramahansa Yogananda," said Paul. "He was believed to be a man of miracles. He cured Yogananda of cholera when Yogananda was a boy."

Our guide grinned and pointed, saying: "Lahiri Mahasaya's home is just a short walk from the shore. And now his home is a shrine, a place where visitors can go. Do you wish to go there?"

"Yes, indeed!" Paul answered.

I was keen on going there, too.

On the way, our guide looked at Paul and smiled, saying "He is calling you! He knows you are here and wants you to visit him!"

Perhaps so! Except that Lahiri Mahasaya passed away about a century ago!

Our guide took us quickly to the shore. We arrived at a dock and our team got out, following our guide up the steps of the ghats and into a narrow walkway between buildings. At a distance of perhaps one hundred fifty meters or so from the shore, our guide turned left into a corridor and there was a door. He rang a buzzer and a rather short and frail but cheerful elderly lady in a sari met us. She was the caretaker, and she invited us to enter the courtyard of the dwelling. There was a small, separate stone structure which houses a beautiful, white marble bust of Lahiri Mahasaya. Also, a crypt of his ashes was in the shrine. Paul and I bowed and sat down on the stone floors to pray and meditate. We asked our Indian team members to talk with the caretaker and explain to her about our filming project.

Each of us was overcome with a strange sensation. We had set out for India partially because Paramahansa Yogananda, who passed

A statue of Lahiri Mahasaya near the urn with his ashes

away in 1952, had insisted in his writings that the three Magi or Wise Men of the *Gospel of Matthew* were from India, and that Jesus had returned their visit. Paul and Anil had gone to Yogananda's Self-Realization Fellowship Mother Center at Mount Washington in Los Angeles specifically to ask for Yogananda's protection and blessings for this journey. There at the Mother Center, behind the chair in which the great guru had sat to lead so many in meditation while he was alive, were pictures of the men recognized as gurus by SRF.

Each of those gurus had somehow impacted upon our journey. Those gurus included Jesus Christ, and it was the search for the Missing Years and untold parts of the life of Jesus that had beckoned us here, so far from home. Krishna was another of the gurus, and we had paid homage to him at ISKCON, witnessing the statue of Krishna covered with gems, diamonds, emeralds and rubies. The other four pictures of the gurus at Mount Washington were Babaji, Lahiri Mahasaya, Swami Sri Yukteswar and Yogananda.

Babaji had flashed into our vision as a poster in the window of a three-wheeled taxi, and then in Kolkata Paul had touched a trident said to have been once given to Yogananda by Babaji. As for Yogananda, we had visited the neighborhood of his childhood, and Paul had talked at length to a relative of Tulsi Bose, who had been a childhood friend of Yogananda seen in photographs with him. As for Swami Sri Yukteswar, we had visited his ashram in Puri and had been permitted to enter the shrine that held his mortal remains.

There was only one of these six gurus we had not yet paid homage to on our trip, and that was Lahiri Mahasaya. We did not know where in India he had lived. For some reason we had not given thought to that. We had left him out. And it so happened that at the one time his name came up in our conversation, out of the entire vast nation of India, the house that contained his remains was close enough to us that we could see it, that yellow house with the flag up on the hill above the ghats.

It defied reason. It was simply incredible. And now we had been admitted to the house to see his statue and to kneel before the urn that contained his remains. (Normally, "ascended masters" are not cremated among the Hindus, however, advanced yogis who are "householders" are subject to cremation. Lahiri Mahasaya had been married with sons and was therefore a "householder yogi.")

In our imagination, it was as though the spirit of Lahiri Mahasaya was saying to us, "you will not leave me out, on this voyage! You will not come to India and pay your respects to five of the six masters and not come to me. I bring you to me. At the very moment you mentioned me you were close by my home, and through the boatman and guide I caused you to turn your heads toward my home and then to climb the steps of the ghats and enter this house. This is made right, now. We accept the respect you have now shown to the six of us. Go now in peace."

But such things are simply not possible. Are they?

Before leaving, we made a donation and then returned to our hotel for some rest.

A DRAMATIC FIRE CEREMONY

After lunch in the air-conditioned restaurant of our hotel, most of us took a nap in our rooms. I had a bit of an upset stomach. Since I was not essential for filming that afternoon, I took some medicine and stayed in the room to rest.

Paul said that he and the rest of the team would go back to the Ganges and film from a boat again. I wished them luck and stayed in bed.

Around sunset, I got up and put on clean clothes. Then I returned to the hotel restaurant and had a light dinner. I tried to choose safe foods which I thought would digest well and keep my stomach happy.

I then returned to the room and took some more medicine. As is typical in many hotels in India, there was no television in the room.

I looked in my luggage and found my small Bell & Howell shortwave radio. It operated on batteries. I extended the antenna and soon picked up the BBC World Service. It was good to catch up on the news.

About 10:30 or so that night, Paul and the rest of the team returned. They were in high spirits and told me they had just finished filming a dramatic fire ceremony. (That ceremony became the very opening shot of **"Jesus in India"** and was also used to begin the end credits.)

The ceremony took place at night, on the ghats beside the river. Paul and his helpers were filming from the boat we had used earlier; the boatman kept the boat as steady as possible at a very calm part of the river. The ceremony involved flaming torches, clanging cymbals and a large crowd. The result, they said, was spectacular! I was certainly convinced when I later saw the footage.

I congratulated them, and then I soon went to sleep for the night. I had had enough excitement for one day, and I was still recovering from an upset stomach.

On my first trip to India, I had met with some Hindu scholars in Varanasi who told me about an ancient Healing Arts School. That school had existed, they said, 2,000 years ago in Varanasi.

Legend has it that at one time young Jesus had gone to study there. There is even some folklore that Jesus may have learned how to remove eye cataracts using obsidian blades. At the present time, we could not track down any leads regarding that information. Our schedule pressed us forward. I hope to research that information more in the future. It was on my mind, however, that some of Jesus' healing of the blind might have been through training in India to use obsidian blades for cataract surgery. The people in Judea would simply not have understood that he was using natural means, with which they were not familiar, to effect those cures. Another day, another theory.

When Binny heard the theory, of course he laughed.

Paul Davids (right) with assistant director Binny on the Ganges

10. Bareilly, New Delhi and Agra

"Tata dharma
Yata jaya."
(Where there is righteousness,
there is victory)
---saying from India

In the morning, we had a light breakfast at the hotel restaurant. We then walked to a nearby bank and changed some U.S. money into Indian rupees. After that, we returned to our hotel and packed our bags. Then we checked out of the Gautam Hotel and loaded into two yellow taxis en route to the train station. Our next destination would be Bareilly!

Thank God that our train this time had air conditioning!

We relaxed as it pulled out of the crowded Varanasi Train Station. As we later rolled through the farmlands and open fields, Paul and I talked about how well our filming was going.

"And you remember," said Paul, "about the Hindu priest in Madurai who mentioned Father Baptiste?"

"That's right," I replied. "He said that Father Baptiste is the Catholic Bishop at Bareilly, and that he may have some knowledge about Jesus in India."

As we gazed out the windows of the train at the fields and simple huts of farming communities, we often saw farmers in traditional clothing using oxen and wooden plows. Paul and I remarked that perhaps some of the everyday scenes would have looked the same 2,000 years ago. Amazing to think about.

We arrived later that day in Bareilly, a moderate-sized city in north-central India. Sanjay had arranged for us to stay at a fairly nice, modern hotel just across the avenue from the train station. Our porters at the train station loaded our baggage onto three horse-drawn carts, or "tongas."

The tonga drivers took us across the parking area and avenue to the Bareilly Towers. Since being in Varanasi, we had been joined by Anil's cousin, Rajneesh Charan, from New Delhi. As the reader will recall, when I first arrived on this trip at Delhi, Rajneesh had met me at the airport. It was good to see him again. He had lived in Bareilly before moving to New Delhi, and he helped us now to check into the hotel.

Also, Rajneesh had arranged a little India-America goodwill party for our arrival. The hotel porters helped us carry our baggage up to our rooms, and we unpacked and cleaned up. The rooms had pleasant furnishings this time, but again, no television. I told myself that I would not, in the future, take television for granted!

The porters brought up trays of snacks and about eight large bottles of ice-cold beer and glasses. In about half an hour, our guests arrived and we had a jolly time.

Paul led us in a toast to "Indian-American friendship and goodwill". We had a lively discussion about our Jesus in India research and filming. I later slept like a brick.

INTERVIEW WITH FATHER BAPTISTE

About seven the next morning, the doorbell rang and a porter arrived with steaming, hot tea and biscuits. After a shave and shower, I got dressed and was soon ready to see Father Baptiste, who had agreed to allow us to interview him. We all boarded into two yellow taxis.

I heard from Madhu that some of our team members that morning would be looking for an owner of a Himalayan bear, because we wanted to have some footage, if possible, of a dancing bear. Not that it had anything to do with our central theme. But it would have been useful ambience for conveying India, which is known not only for its temple elephants and snake charmers but also its dancing bears.

At some places in northern India, a wandering man will have a semi-tame bear with a collar and chain. The bear will, on command, stand up and dance. The owner collects donations for the entertainment. I suggested that perhaps we might film this concerning a humorous song lyric. The serious song lyric is: "Gladly the cross I'd bear." As a child growing up in fundamentalist Christianity, I had sometimes seen local wags change the words and meaning, writing: "'Gladly', the cross-eyed bear."

This time, the bears were all out of town.

We arrived at the Catholic Church where Father Baptiste works. He and a fellow priest met us cordially at the entrance. Rajneesh had once been a parishioner of Father Baptiste. In fact, Rajneesh was yet

Ed Martin (left) with Father Baptiste (right)

another member of our team who was not a Hindu and who was a
Christian, a Catholic actually, and he was sincere in his beliefs and
practices. It was remarkable the extent to which he was helping us
with our project. Perhaps he felt Father Baptiste could set us right,
where we had gone wrong. However, Father Baptiste was very well
aware of the legends of Jesus in India and had even heard them while
in seminary school, especially that Jesus had traveled to Kashmir.

Paul said that the lighting conditions outside were perfect right
then and suggested we start filming immediately. We brought chairs
outside, in front of the church building, and began the interview.

Reproduced below I have presented the section of the interview
that appears in **"Jesus in India,"** verbatim:

FATHER BAPTISTE:
Jesus didn't start a religion. Jesus started a way of life —that is
away from the way of life of Pharisees and Scribes— Matthew
5:20 — unless your religiosity is deeper than the religiosity of

the Scribes and Pharisees, you will not enter the Kingdom of Heaven. And what Jesus wanted — that everyone enter the Kingdom of Heaven — experience God as the Father. As far as the Missing Years or lost years, I believe — I take it that Jesus was there in Israel, in the family. It is quite possible that St. Joseph, being an elderly man, must have died— and the responsibility fell upon Jesus to take care of his mother, Mary, and maybe other children. Being eldest, it was his responsibility.

EDWARD T. MARTIN:

Father, part of my research about the missing time in the life of Jesus is concerning a Russian explorer named Nicolas Notovitch. And in 1887 he was in Ladakh at the Hemis Monastery, and at that time he became friends with the Buddhist lamas. And after some time they trusted him, and they told him they had a 2000 year old document that tells about Jesus in India, about the missing time in the life of Jesus, and that document is called **The Life of St. Issa, the Best of the Sons of Men**. And it has a lot of details. And I am wondering, have you ever met anyone here in India who has ever talked about that document or that information?

FATHER BAPTISTE:

I have heard that Jesus was in Kashmir. The talk was there, and it goes long back. From one of the students in the seminary I have heard that Jesus was in Kashmir— that Jesus came to Kashmir — that is, and I still believe it to be, just a rumor without any historicity or any proof on that.

EDWARD T. MARTIN:

We have a saying in English, where there's smoke there's fire. And we don't know but where there's a rumor, sometimes there's a little bit of truth.

Father Baptiste is a charming man, and he gave a wonderful interview. He invited us to return later in the afternoon for filming of the evening church service.

We returned and beforehand got some excellent footage of the local wild monkeys. The monkeys took cookies from our hands and

Father Baptiste, Bishop of Bareilly,
lived in a house with beautiful grounds

did some delightful antics! There were also large fruit bats flying around the churchyard, and some landed in the tall trees.

Paul filmed the service, and afterwards, we thanked Father Baptiste and his helpers, made a donation and left.

PAUL'S MAGIC SHOW!

We freshened up a little at our hotel and then we all boarded two horse-drawn tongas and headed out. We went to a house a few blocks away, where Paul had agreed to put on a magic show for a group of children and adults.

We arrived and did our best to power up the amount of light in a medium-sized room. Perhaps fifteen to twenty children arrived and about ten adults. Paul told me later that he intentionally wears a long-sleeved shirt to such events. He said that people always expect a magician to "have something up his sleeve," even though he never does.

He likes to fuel the suspicion. And he can at times dramatically roll up his sleeves to focus the attention of the audience. The show involved playing cards, coins, glasses, cloth and so on. I was impressed! And so was the audience! Everyone applauded enthusiastically at the end of the performance.

Next, several adults came into the room carrying trays with bottles of of cold Pepsi with drinking straws, ice cream treats and cookies. Rajneesh had invited everyone and made the preparations.

A HIGH SPEED TRAIN BOARDING

My alarm went off at six a.m., and I quickly got up, shaved and dressed. I finished packing and met Paul in the front lobby at about twenty minutes before seven a.m. Our express train to New Delhi would leave the station at seven a.m. sharp. The front of our hotel was only about one hundred fifty meters away from the entrance to the train station. Our Indian team members were supposed to meet us at about a quarter to seven. A helpful hotel employee brought us cups of hot tea and cookies on a tray as we sat in the lobby.

By ten minutes before seven, Paul and I were getting antsy. We carried our baggage outside, to the foot of the steps at the entrance, where vehicles could pull up. Paul couldn't reach anyone on his cell phone. We walked closer to the front gate. The minutes were ticking away and we were not at the station. It began to seem definite we would miss the train.

At five minutes before seven a.m., at long last two yellow taxis came screeching up. We jumped in with our team, speeding over to the train station as fast as they could drive. We piled out with all of our

Racing to make the train

bags, and about half a dozen train porters helped us. We all literally ran, as fast as we could, into the station, up the stairs of the overpassage to our express train, waiting on a far track. Binny did everything in his power to help Anil, who walked with his cane, and then at the last minute Binny lifted Anil and carried him onto the train.

As we had all been scrambling to pick up our thirteen pieces of baggage, a strong, cheerful man who looked like a holy sadhu with an orange turban had offered his help. He quickly grabbed heavy pieces of luggage and ran swiftly with us, grinning all the time. We ran down the stairs from the overpassage ramp and quickly put everything aboard the train.

As I stepped onto the train, I said "Thank you!" to the beaming sadhu. I glanced down only a second to take a ten-rupee note from my pocket and held it out as an offering, smiling. But the sadhu had vanished, as if into thin air! And the platform was almost empty. How could he possibly have gotten away so quickly? Inexplicable and uncanny things like that often seemed to happen to us in India.

The train whistle blew at that second and we lurched forward. I had to grab a handrail to keep from falling. We all quickly found our seats as the train picked up speed.

"By the way," said Paul, "didn't we see that sadhu before? The man in white clothes with the orange turban and a neatly trimmed beard?"

"Yes," I replied, "I think he helped us at another train station once before."

"I don't believe it," said Paul, always the Doubting Thomas. "It couldn't have been the same man."

"I know it couldn't have been," I replied, "but I'm sure it was."

"Did you tip him?" asked Paul.

"I tried to, but he just disappeared, like one of your magic tricks!"

RETURN TO NEW DELHI

We arrived later in New Delhi, but we found out that for some reason we could not check into our room at the International Inn until about six p.m. We temporarily took all our things and went to the waiting room at the New Delhi Train Station. The large room was crowded with Indian people and had no air conditioning. The air was fetid and miserably hot. Anil said he had a nauseous stomach again and that he, Binny, and Madhu would go to Rajneesh's apartment to rest and cool off. Paul and I found ourselves essentially volunteering to wait with our baggage in the sweltering, hot waiting room. Then Paul got an idea.

Paul said, "While you go to Rajneesh's apartment, maybe Ed and I can check into an air conditioned hotel nearby for a few hours."

Anil replied that he was sure that there were no air conditioned hotels anywhere near the train station. But in this case he was wrong. I told Paul that years ago I had stayed at a modestly priced air conditioned hotel within a two-minute walk of the train station. I couldn't recmember the name, but I knew how to get there. I asked Paul to look at his watch: "I'll go there, get us an air conditioned room, and I'll be back within ten minutes!"

"Okay" said Paul.

I took off at a run, leaving Paul to guard our baggage. At the train station entrance I instantly got a driver with a three-wheeled scooter taxi and said: "Step on it! Go fast! This way!"

I pointed the directions and we quickly raced off. It was a rapid trip; we only had to go about two hundred to three hundred meters. We were on a side street called Dariba Pan, in front of the train station. I ran in, negotiated an air conditioned room until six p.m., got the key and left. I had asked the scooter driver to wait; we sped off.

I paid and tipped the driver and raced inside. I smiled and showed Paul the key. "You made it with a few seconds to spare," Paul said with a grin.

We picked up our baggage and got into the same scooter taxi I had just used. The hotel was called: Millennium 2000 DX Hotel at 3695 Dariba Pan (opposite Shiela Cinema). We took showers, put on clean clothes and took a nap, enjoying the cool air.

"We have to plan a time to film at the Taj Mahal," Paul said.

"Actually, Madhu suggested we go there tomorrow," I explained.

Later in the afternoon, we called Madhu's cell phone and told where we could be picked up.

We all went in two yellow taxis to the International Inn, located near the New Delhi Airport, on National Highway. The rooms were pretty tiny, but they did have one color television in the lobby.

Now if one thing is certain it's that Jesus never saw the Taj Mahal. It was conceived and built so long after the era of Christ that we had no research purpose to make the trip there. However everyone watching any film about India expects to see the Taj Mahal. We needed to go there to shoot footage of it, as Paul figured it could be useful for the opening credits. (That, in fact, is where the footage was used.)

And so the next morning, at some God-awful time around four a.m., we all got up and boarded a tour bus going to Agra, to see the Taj Mahal.

A DREAM IN STONE: THE TAJ MAHAL

I did some napping on the bus; it was air conditioned and fairly pleasant. Years ago, on my first trip to India, I had visited the Taj Mahal. It was a marvelous experience! I had also at that time stopped in Agra at a sitar shop and paid for a beautiful sitar and the shipping to the USA. The sitar never arrived! I thought about going to the shop, but who other than me would remember that I had been ripped off about thirty years before? So I pushed that thought from my mind. And we were on a tight schedule. But just for the record, I am still owed that blasted sitar!

The weather that day was constantly cloudy and very hot and humid. The time I was there before, the season was autumn and the weather was much cooler and sunnier. Also, for some reason this time,

A crowd of visitors at the Taj Mahal

a small and very persistent group of street vendor boys followed us, trying to sell postcards. They would not give up, no matter what we did.

I lack words to express just how little I wanted to buy postcards. If they had been free and thrown in my face, I would have dodged them and let them fall to the pavement.

Finally, Madhu and Binny spoke loudly and angrily in Hindi and the boys gave up, snarling at us as they retreated.

To see the Taj, visitors pay for an admission ticket which for non-Indians was then five hundred rupees (about ten dollars USA). On my first visit, I believe the admission was less than twenty-five cents. But who could complain? For ten dollars one certainly gets one's money's worth to see one of the Seven Wonders of the World!

Visitors to the Taj Mahal pass through a darkened stone room to enter the courtyard. The first view everyone has of the Taj is through a single portal which gives a direct, straight alignment of the reflecting pool with the dome. It is a dramatic view! Many people raise their hands and gasp as they approach the portal.

The Taj Mahal is spectacular, and the gardens are sublime, but after two or three hours, frankly, I was ready for a Kingfisher beer and a nap. Go figure!

Producer Anil Urmil (left), the author and Rajneesh Charan (right), exhausted but thrilled to be at the Taj Mahal

11. Dharamsala, Pathankot, and Amritsar

A poor village woman in ancient India suffered greatly, trying to care for her disabled husband and small children. One day, Lord Shiva, in the disguise of a wandering holy man, visited her village. The woman gave the holy man all of the coins she had earned that day gathering firewood. "Help me," she implored, "to have abundant wealth that I may care for my husband and children."

Shiva, moved by her act of faith, went to the heavenly realm and met with his son, Ganesha. "Her karma," said Ganesha, "is not good enough. I cannot grant her wealth."

"I am not asking," said Shiva, "I am demanding. If you do not grant her wealth, I will do it myself and then give you a good thrashing!"

"Father, don't go wild with me again!" said Ganesha. He then turned all the leaves of the tree in front of the poor woman's hut into solid gold. The woman and her family gathered the leaves and all lived the rest of their lives in abundance.

---Hindu folk story

We left New Delhi the next morning with a hired driver who came with an air-conditioned SUV. We were headed for Dharamsala, in the province of Himachal Pradesh, in the Himalayan foothills. Dharamsala (actually upper Dharamsala, which is called McLeod Ganj) is the home of His Holiness the 14th Dalai Lama (Tenzin Gyatso), who fled Tibet in the 1950's when the Chinese Communists invaded. The Dalai Lama is head of the Gelugpa, or Yellow Hat, sect of Tibetan Buddhism and is revered as Tibet's god-king. India has graciously granted sanctuary to the Dalai Lama. Thousands of other Tibetan refugees live at Dharamsala and elsewhere in India, Nepal, and Bhutan.

On my first trip to India in the 1970's, I visited Dharamsala and was enchanted by the entire atmosphere: the scenery, the wonderful Tibetan people and their rich cultural and spiritual heritage. When we were first planning our filming project in the spring of 2005, I strongly suggested that we include Dharamsala in our itinerary. If nothing else,

A Hindu shaman holding a Shiva trident in Dharamsala

we could get some great shots of the Himalayan scenery and the Tibetan people and buildings. And of course, it would have been splendid to see the Dalai Lama.

The dense cloud cover continued throughout our journey as we gained elevation, going northward into the province of Himachal Pradesh. It was the height of the monsoon season, and we had been fortunate to have avoided any torrential rains thus far. However, we

Entrance building leading to the Dalai Lama's compound in Dharamsala

knew we would have some deluges at some point. Paul had told me that he actually wanted at least one filming scene with heavy, torrential rain. The sky looked promising!

FACE TO FACE WITH THE DALAI LAMA

We made a long, winding drive going gradually upward. The scenery transitioned from farmlands to small trees. Then, finally, in the higher elevations we entered a forest of beautiful, tall conifer trees. We were in Himachal Pradesh, in the foothills of the Himalayas.

During the 1800's and early 1900's, the British Viceroys would sometimes come here to Dharamsala to spend the summers. By doing that, they were able to escape the sweltering heat of the lowlands to the south. I knew that one of the Viceroys, Lord Elgin, was buried near mMcLeod Ganj, in the cemetery of the Church of St. John in the Wilderness.

Early in the afternoon, we arrived at Dharamsala and parked our SUV near the center of town. My mind was filled with vivid memories of when I was there before, in the 1970's. Since we had no immediate filming schedule, I told the others that I just wanted to walk alone for a while and have my private thoughts. Everything now was so much more crowded with buildings and people. I walked around slowly, looking everywhere. People, I thought, can so easily forget the past – whether it is directly lived or just read about.

In ten minutes or so, Binny found me and came running up, filled with excitement.

"In about twenty minutes the Dalai Lama will be speaking to a gathering at the monastery right here," he said. "We are not allowed to film, but we can all attend. Are you interested?"

"Yes, indeed!" I replied, and we both took off running.

At the monastery, we passed throught metal detectors and were frisked. We joined the rest of our team who were waiting in a garden area. I happened to be looking around in all directions and noticed a structure in the distance.

I pointed that way and said: "Years ago when I was here, that was the residence of the Dalai Lama. There used to be a sign in front that said that. Apparently, the sign was removed for security reasons. But perhaps he still lives there?"

We all decided to walk in that direction, and then we stood beside the walkway, near the entrance of the house.

At 1:25 p.m. the large door of the house opened and out stepped His Holiness the Dalai Lama, along with an entourage of about ten people. The group included two armed security guards, who flanked the Dalai Lama on either side. They looked like Indian Army personnel and were holding what appeared to be British Sten Guns, a kind of submachine gun. We all smiled, made the namaste gesture with palms together and wished him "Happy Birthday!" July 6th 2005 he was seventy years old.

He smiled at us, returned the gesture and continued on with his group to give the lecture. He appeared warm and genuine, and he acknowledged us kindly. For us, it was a happy experience, especially for producer Anil Urmil, who was able to shake the Dalai Lama's hand and briefly tell him we had journeyed from the United States in hopes of seeing him. There was no possibility of engaging him in conversation then, however, and it would take many months for us to begin a communication with his office to inquire about Jesus in India.

Eventually, after great effort for half a year, Paul succeeded in getting permission to include some statements by the Dalai Lama in our film, which appear close to the ending. There were about a dozen emails back and forth leading up to the permission. The Dalai Lama was very sensitive about speaking out about the subject of Jesus in India, and through a spokesman he professed that the first time he had heard of this was when researchers first posed the question to him. This was to imply that he had no special knowledge of the subject, and that any suggestions that he had seen the missing documents in Tibet when he was a boy were not accurate. Therefore, the statements by monks at the Hemis Monastery, that the Dalai Lama may have had "inside information" about the Nicolas Notovitch document, and may have actually seen the original at a monastery in Tibet, would receive no confirmation, to our disappointment. However, the Dalai Lama did approve our inclusion of some of his pronouncements about the necessity of creating unity and cooperation among the world's great religions, and how religious harmony among religions is essential for world progress.

We thought back to the statements of the Shankaracharya, about how political the "business" of religion is in the world of today. He had stated directly that there are cover-ups related to the ancient knowledge. The blackout of information about the contents of the Dead Sea Scrolls, for decades, was enough to demonstrate that. Perhaps the statement we received from the Dalai Lama would not prove to be the last word. His very security was to some extent dependent upon the United States, which at that time under the government of George Bush was heavily influenced by fundamentalist or "Born Again" Christians. Someone in his position would not be at liberty to reveal something that orthodox Christians might not favor being released or discussed. This was speculation, of course, but there was still the nagging feeling, even up to the publication of this book and the release of **"Jesus in India,"** that we have not by any means heard the the truth, the whole truth and nothing but the truth (so help me God!)

THE CHURCH OF ST. JOHN IN THE WILDERNESS

We decided to drive to a nearby location which I had visited years ago. Driving downhill a short distance from upper Dharamsala (McLeod Ganj) through a beautiful forest of tall conifer trees, we reached the Church of St. John in the Wilderness.

This is a wonderful stone chapel among the trees, with impressive Belgian stained glass windows. This location is high on the mountainside and has a sweeping view. Since it was built in 1852, many notable

Indian and British Christians have worshipped there. The chapel is located below McLeod Ganj, on the road to Kotwali Bazaar.

Inside, the atmosphere is tranquil and historic. The commemorative plaques on the walls have words like: "Royal Bengal Lancers" and "Her Majesty's Gurkha Rifles." To me, the entire mood of the chapel is very spiritual and reflective. I hoped we could convey some of this on film.

Interestingly, as we drove up to the vicinity of the chapel and parked our SUV, the heavens opened up as a torrent of heavy rain began falling. Paul would have his deluge for filming, if he wanted it!

Sitting in the back seat, I gripped my big, sturdy monsoon umbrella and said: "Paul, I'm game for this if you are!"

Paul looked at Binny, who smiled, pulled on his rain poncho and said: "I'm ready!"

Paul got his umbrella ready also, and the three of us stepped slowly out of the SUV into the downpour. I was glad I was wearing my sturdy bison-leather cowboy boots, also. At least the wind wasn't too bad! We walked slowly and deliberately along the footpath as rivulets of streaming water went past our feet. The rain smell was great! I believe it is called a negative ion atmosphere. As fate would have it, several cows were grazing beside the chapel, in the midst of the downpour.

Director Paul Davids prepared to film in a raging downpour

We set up the tripod and filmed footage of the cows and the chapel amid the trees. The whole atmosphere was magical and somehow surreal. "You can't buy this! It's fantastic!" said Paul, in a loud voice, to be heard above the roar of the rain.

A PLACE OF SANCTUARY FROM THE STORM

Just inside the covered entranceway of the church, we took refuge from the storm. We set up the camera tripod, positioned the video camera and continued filming. Paul had the camera facing outside as I stood in silhoutte. From inside the chapel an Indian clergyman approached us. On his own initiative, Binny went over to the minister and diplomatically explained what we were doing. He told us later that he began speaking in Hindi but switched to Gujerati when he realized that was the priest's native language.

As we filmed, the cascade of rain seemed to get even stronger. It certainly was a peculiar, introspective moment, with the majestic forest of tall conifer trees, the quiet, darkened chapel with the beautiful stained glass windows and the pouring torrent of rain. It really was hypnotic in its own way. At some point in the filming, I just decided to stop saying anything. To just look around, listen and to reflect on my thoughts. Time, for a while, seemed to stand still. And at just those moments, the poor cows decided that they had had quite enough of this indignity. They started trodding, one hoof at a time, through the massive downpour, slowly making their way toward shelter.

Paul and I decided to speak in English with the minister who was very gracious. We took a little tour within the chapel and a flood of happy memories came back to me.

About that time, the downpour stopped suddenly. We walked out to the entranceway, peering outside. The silence was somehow strange.

We gave a donation to the clergyman and thanked him. We walked carefully back to the SUV.

Back in Dharamsala, we stayed at the Hotel Highland Bhagsu at Bhagsu Nag. A heavy cloud cover remained and drizzling rain began late in the afternoon.

I sat in a plastic chair on the covered balcony of the room, listening to the news on my shortwave radio and writing. I was thankful to be sheltered from the rain!

The author at Buddhist prayer wheels near the home of the Dalai Lama

ONWARD TO PATHANKOT

After buying some wonderful Tibetan souvenirs in some of the Tibetan-owned shops, we left in mid-morning. I had bought a couple of beautiful thangka paintings on cloth scrolls, some postcards (yes, I was back in the postcard buying business now that we had left the Taj Mahal), and a Tibetan necklace for a lady friend. My favorite of those postcards shows the Dalai Lama's face, the North Face of Mt. Everest, and the Potala Palace in Lhasa. It is a heroic, victorious-looking picture. (I keep it on my refrigerator to remind me of the ongoing, heroic struggle of the valiant Tibetan people.)

Some distance down the mountainside, in the vicinity of lower Dharamsala, we stopped for a rest break. Oddly enough, we looked beside us and found a Hindu-operated rest home for old cows! Amazing, but true!

The gentleman who is the caretaker lovingly makes sure the cows always have feed, water, and shelter. Holy animals deserve respect, according to Hindus, even to the end of their lives.

In fact, Anil informed us that there are wealthy Hindus who support such rest homes for aged cows to live out their natural lives, which left me wondering if they outnumbered the rest homes for elderly people!

En route to Pathankot, we came upon a truly gigantic statue of the beloved monkey-deity of the Hindus, Hanuman, who as I mentioned is a hero of the ancient, epic poem, **The Ramayana.**

A huge statue of Hanuman, the Hindu Monkey-Deity,
that we passed on the way to Pathankot

Close to sunset, we arrived in the small city of Pathankot in northwestern India. I had visited there before, on my first trip to India. I had taken a bus from Pathankot to reach Dharamsala that time. Now, we were to visit Anil's brother, Avenash, who was a medical doctor serving in the Indian Army.

We all got together at the rooftop cafe of the hotel where we were staying, Hotel Venice on Dhangu Road in Pathankot. Avenash hosted a dinner for us later that evening. Everyone had a great time.

The next morning we briefly visited Avenash at the Indian Army Base where he works at Pathankot. He had a soldier bring in hot tea

*Dr. Avinash Urmil, who helped coordinate
our production travels in nothern India*

and cookies for us. We visited for a while, looked at our watches and
then had to be on our way. We thanked him for his hospitality and
headed on the road again.

We passed through an extensive area of fields and farmlands: the
rich, agricultural region of Punjab. We were on our way to visit a marvelous, magical place which I had gone to on my first journey to India.

THE GOLDEN TEMPLE OF THE SIKHS

The name of this province: "Punjab" means "Panch" (five) and
"ab" (waters or rivers). "The Land of the Five Rivers" is referred to in
the movie **"The Ten Commandments."**

When an envoy to the Pharoah unfurls a length of red silk, the
Queen remarks, "It shimmers like the Nile! What is it?"

The envoy replies: "It comes from the Land of the Five Rivers;
some say it is woven on the looms of the gods. It is called silk."

As we know, silk actually came from eastern China, but its path of
commerce was the legendary "Silk Road." And that ancient caravan
route passed through Punjab on its way westward, all the way to the
Mediterranean!

Probably several of the researchers of Jesus in India have passed
through Amritsar and visited the Golden Temple, which is pictured on
the cover of this book and the poster for our film. At least one was

Nicolas Notovitch, who visited in 1887. He was impressed by the structure, and he wrote about it in his book: ***The Unknown Life of Jesus Christ***.

The city where the Golden Temple is located is Amritsar, which means "pool of nectar." The temple is situated in the middle of a large pool of water, about the size of four football fields. A single, stone walkway connects the stone perimeter to the temple.

We had a good lunch at a popular restaurant and then asked our SUV driver to park his vehicle. As usual, the driver stayed constantly with his vehicle, guarding it and never getting more that several feet away.

Our team boarded two bicycle rickshaws which wound through narrow streets and finally reached an open plaza. The entrance area to the Golden Temple!

We checked in our footwear at a spacious stone building in front of the entrance. Cheerful, turbaned Sikh men accepted our shoes and gave us each a round, claim token. They seemed particularly amused at my tall, bison-leather cowboy boots! They smiled at each other and showed them around a little, as if to say: "We don't see this very often!"

Paul wears a head-cloth and goes barefoot
so he can film at the Golden Temple

From a smiling boy, we bought large, orange-colored cloth handkerchiefs to tie around the tops of our heads. Having some kind of head covering is required. Also, we bought small bundles of flowers as offerings. Then, up the steps at the entrance, we washed our feet in a constant flow of clean, clear water. We were ready!

Paul held the video camera, and we moved slowly under the stone archway. "Oh! My God!" someone said breathlessly. (And yes, the Golden Temple is covered with plating made of real gold, covering every inch.)

Glistening in the afternoon sun, the Golden Temple was right in front of us! I had been there before, but I was still awestruck for a while; it is truly an astonishing place. Paul remarked later that he was actually more impressed by the Golden Temple than by the Taj Mahal!

What makes the Golden Temple such a special place? I believe it is the strongly spiritual atmosphere which permeates the entire temple area. Also, there is a very positive, cheerful, and yes, wholesome attitude given out by everyone. The "sankalpa" or totality of consciousness is very good!

I went with the flow of Sikh pilgrims down the walkway, into the Golden Temple, just as I did years ago. A wonderful experience! And later I wandered leisurely around the entire perimeter of the pool. I was holding my camera at the ready, looking for magical scenes. And there were dozens of them. Sikhs, male and female, cheerfully performed a variety of duties, doing such things as cleansing the marble walkways with water. There were long lines of colorfully dressed Sikhs, waiting to enter the temple itself, where chants and prayers were being broadcast to be heard not only by all on the temple grounds, but also for people many blocks away in the town itself.

The Golden Temple of the Sikhs is one of the great wonders of northern India

After spending most of the afternoon there, we looked at our watches and remembered that Anil wanted us to see another special sight: the changing of the India-Pakistan border guards!

TO THE BORDER OF PAKISTAN

The time was about 4:30 in the afternoon, and we were racing along in our SUV, westbound from Amritsar. We were on the paved, two-lane road which goes west to the border with Pakistan at a place called Wagah. I had crossed right through that spot in the 1970's coming overland from Pakistan, on my first trip to India. We sped through the open farmlands, sometimes seeing industrious Sikh farmers driving modern tractors in their fields. There is a picture like that on some of the Indian currency.

Approaching the border, we saw many vehicles and hundreds of Indian people. Most of them appeared to be families with women and children. Our driver parked his vehicle, took a restroom break and returned. We had gotten our camera gear and other equipment ready. Our driver, as always, guarded his vehicle, and the rest of us walked to the border.

When I was there before, in the 1970's, customs officials worked out of a few simple, wooden huts. Now, there are modern brick and stone buildings and flower beds. Also, there is a massive, stone entranceway to India through which the road passes. And there are fairly high, sturdy bleachers on both sides of the road, close to the customs buildings. The bleachers were filling up with people to watch the changing of the guard ceremony.

Years ago, when I passed through here, coming overland from Pakistan, the bus stopped a short distance away. Passengers had to walk about two hundred meters through a "no man's land" to reach the India side. At that time, there was considerable hostility between India and Pakistan. Also on that day, a long, snaking line of porters were carrying boxes of grapes on their heads, unloading from trucks on one side and loading trucks on the other.

THE CHANGING OF THE GUARDS

A trumpet blew and an Indian Army officer loudly gave some commands in Hindi. The young soldiers were all very tall and smartly dressed in ceremonial uniforms. Their turbans had ornate, multi-colored fans at the top. The soldiers clicked their heels in unison and began marching toward the gate. On the other side, the also very tall Pakistani guards (with their own impressive stone structures nearby) began marching. The Pakistani soldiers wore mostly dark uniforms with turbans.

A very energetic, smiling Indian woman in a sari sprang from the crowd of spectators on the Indian side, into the paved road. Stirring, patriotic music began playing on loudspeakers. The woman began a lively, patriotic dance in the road, twirling and swaying to the music.

"Jai Hind!"(Hail India!) she boomed.

"Jai Hind!" the audience roared back.

She really put on a great dance show. She held a long piece of colorful cloth in her hands which fluttered and moved as she spun and swayed. A beautiful sunset was taking place to the west, on the Pakistani side.

CHOICE FILMING LOCATIONS

Meanwhile, Paul and company had adroitly managed to set up the tripod and video camera in ideal places. Suddenly officials approached them, asking for production passes which we did not have. It looked as though we were going to be escorted away, when abruptly Anil Urmil mentioned something about his brother, who is an Indian Army officer, to the military officer in charge. They recognized Anil's brothers name, and after some quick conversation in which Anil assured them his brother would be very unhappy if Paul returned to Pathankot empty-handed and without the footage, the officer in charge looked over his shoulders, into the crowd, and quickly decided to become very helpful to Paul and Binny. He even took them personally to the best filming spots and told them in advance when key moments of the ceremony were about to begin, so they wouldn't miss anything. (Anil enjoyed this so much he laughed about it for days afterwards.)

I wasn't needed then, so I took one of the high seats in the south bleachers and just enjoyed the show.

I don't recall seeing any other foreigners in the crowd besides Paul and myself. The changing of the guards is mostly an event for the enjoyment of Indian and Pakistani citizens – and rightfully so – it is impressive to watch. And the Indian military is rightfully a source of pride for the Indian people, as the Pakistani military is a source of pride for Pakistanis.

It is so ironic. Pakistan and India are countries in conflict. Each has nuclear weapons. They threaten one another, and there is an active military insurgency in Kashmir. There are even sometimes terrorist actions they take against one another. And yet, they cooperate totally for the changing of the guard and flag lowering ceremony at the end of each day at the border between the two nations. Civilians on each side of the border cheer their soldiers like spectators routing for their team at a football game. It is like a colorful pageant, an enthralling and perfectly choreographed dance between two nations hostile to one another but in a love-hate relationship, each feeling great pride and working together to perfect every brilliant detail of this shared performance at sunset.

What a strange world we live in!

We drove back as darkness fell in Amritsar, and we stayed at the K.R. Resort & Hotel Pvt. Ltd. located at the 7th Mile Stone on Airport Road. It was fancier than anything I needed, but it was okay. It was also almost empty of guests. Our next destination was New Delhi.

For some reason, we were taking a short airplane hop to New Delhi. We had to wake up at some God-awful time around 1:30 a.m. At the Amritsar Airport we boarded an Indian Airlines flight and were soon on our way.

At the flag ceremony at the India-Pakistan border

12. To Kashmir: Into the Den of the Tiger

"To get a tiger's cub,
you must go into the den of a tiger."
---folk saying from India

We stayed again at the International Inn at A-78 National Highway No. 8, Mahipalpur, near the airport in south Delhi.

About mid-day the next day, we had another airplane flight: this time to Srinagar in Kashmir! After all the debate about the dangers for us as Americans to be in Srinagar, the initial plan was that we would fly in for half a day, and that Paul and I would never leave the protection of the airport, while our Hindu crew would film at the tomb of Yuz Asaf, which the Ahmadiyya Muslims acknowledge as the actual tomb of the historical Jesus of Nazareth.

However, the plan quickly changed. We were now to stay in Srinagar one day and then that turned into two. The new plan would have Paul and me remaining secluded at a houseboat on Dal Lake, while our Hindu crew and Binny and Anil went into the Muslim district to accomplish getting footage of the ancient tomb. They would try to conceal the fact that there were Americans at the houseboat (fat chance!), and when Paul and I did need to go into the town for food it would be under cover of darkness. We would go only to a Tibetan restaurant where the owner would be assisting in our protection.

The State Department had issued warnings about such travel, but we decided to try. We didn't have any way to know then that a year after our departure, terrorists would bomb houseboats very close to those where we were staying, reducing the appeal of tourism in Srinagar even more. And just a couple days after our departure from the area near the tomb, twelve civilians and one army officer would be blown up by a bomb. The army officer, we heard, was decapitated by the blast.

With the dangers pushed to the back of our minds, we planned our trip to Srinagar, Kashmir, and we felt that the footage would be a key for what we were trying to accomplish in the film.

For me, this would be the high point of our trip. On my first journey to India, I had traveled by bus to reach Srinagar in the valley of Kashmir. We might have done the same this time, but we had serious security concerns (traveling by road was not safe), and we had time restraints. We needed to fly.

Paul, Binny and Madhu had to do some business at a bank and other errands. So Anil and I headed to the domestic airport to wait for the others. At first, since we did not have our tickets with us, we were not allowed into the air conditioned terminal to wait. I made some inquiries and found we could buy "waiting tickets" for about fifty cents each. So we got out of the sweltering heat and into the cool airport. We also had access to the restrooms and snack bars.

I called Madhu's cell phone to ask about Dnyanesh Moghe, our Indian cameraman who was planning on arriving from Goa to join us on the journey to Srinagar. Madhu said he would arrive at any minute.

I got up from the rows of airport chairs and walked toward the glass entrance doors. Right then, Dnyanesh came walking up.

I excitedly shook his hand and told him I was glad to have him back with us. He said his wife was recovering well from her car accident injuries. I was so delighted to have him back with us. We would need some humor where we were going! And so Dnyanesh took up again his responsibilities as one of our two associate producers for India and as second unit cameraman. However, at the tomb he would not be second unit. It was far too dangerous for Paul, an American, to go there. Dnyanesh would film there by himself.

Anil, Dnyanesh and I sat together to visit a while. I brought us some paper cups of hot tea from the snack bar. DM had some current news from Goa and some pieces of news he had heard from Kashmir: various bombings and acts of violence were continuing.

I told DM how several days ago I had made a long distance phone call and spoken with my old friend, Aziz Kashmiri, the retired newspaper editor I interviewed years ago, the author of **Christ in Kashmir**. He still lived in Srinagar and invited us to visit and interview him. Of course, he lived in a Muslim neighborhood in a city where there was constant tension and frequent violence between Muslims and Hindus. What a sight we would make in his neighborhood, Americans and Hindus walking up to his house.

About then, a cheerful voice said: "Hey guys! How are you?" It was our travel agent and our other associate producer for India, Sanjay Shetye! He had traveled up from Goa to join us and travel to Srinagar. The last time I had seen him was at the beginning of our journey, when we all had a rendezvous at the train station in Goa. Sanjay had helped us countless times on our journey by making travel arrangements; he had always been available by cell phone.

Right then, Paul, Binny, Madhu and Rajneesh walked up with a group of porters carrying their baggage. We had quite a team now! And we were all in high spirits!

THE ADVENTURE OF ADVENTURES

We all proceeded to the check-in counter and got our boarding passes; Sanjay had booked us on Indian Airlines.

Sometimes called "Heaven on Earth," the vale of Kashmir is truly a fantastic place. This was my first return since the 1970's. I was really excited! And I was about to discover that, due to warfare and severe tensions between the Islamic and Hindu communities in Kashmir, the land of "milk and honey" that was Kashmir was no longer peaceful in any respect. The mood there had entirely changed. The fact was that many of the Hindu community had been routed from their homes by the Muslim population. The Indian government was still in control and the military presence was everywhere, but the streets certainly were not safe, especially for foreigners.

A Tibetan restaurant owner helped provide protection for us during our time in Srinagar

The next part of our plans included a flight from Srinagar to Leh in nearby Ladakh. From Leh, we would take a driver and SUV to the Hemis Monastery in an attempt to see the ancient *Life of Saint Issa* document. Or at least, we thought that's what would come next at that time.

Our flight was only about half full, which was fine with me. During the flight, I saw Binny sitting nearby at a window seat alone, looking thoughtfully out the window at the mountains below. "Well, Binny," I said, "what do you think?"

He beamed a wide smile and replied: "This is the adventure of adventures! I can hardly believe that it is really happening!"

"I feel the same way," I responded, "but it is really happening. I feel very grateful to be returning."

"You know it is not Jesus Christ buried in the Tomb of Yuz Asaf, don't you?" said Binny.

"And how do you know that?" I asked with a furrowed brow.

"Because he died, was resurrected and ascended to heaven."

"Does that mean you don't want to visit the tomb?"

"I do want to visit the tomb," he confirmed.

"And why do you want to do that?"

"Because you've proven to me it's a mystery who is buried there. Perhaps it is Saint Thomas?"

"Binny, we visited the tomb of Saint Thomas in Chennai," I said. "Doubting Thomas can't be buried in both places."

Binny nodded thoughtfully and said nothing more.

The Himalayan scenery below was spectacular. For all of us, we were very aware of the possible dangers and risks involved with this part of our journey.

The state of Jammu and Kashmir is the only Muslim majority state in India, and it is by far the most violent part of India. Some Muslim extremists want the province to become part of Pakistan, and of course, India is bitterly opposed to that. Bombings and assassinations take place frequently and several people die every day.

Our flight arrived at the Srinagar Airport without incident. Outside the buildings as well as within, I noticed a remarkable number of well-armed Indian soldiers. They all wore helmets and flack jackets as well as carrying modern automatic rifles. Some of the rifles looked to me like top-of-the-line Belgian-made Fabrique Nationales and others looked like German Heckler & Koch models. No antiquated, early-1900's bolt action rifles for these guys!

TO OUR HOUSEBOAT ON DAL LAKE

We claimed our baggage and somehow managed to all squeeze into a small mini-van. We were just crowded enough to be miserable! Why, I thought, couldn't we have just taken two vehicles? It was a warm, sunny day and the vehicle had no air conditioning.

I rolled down a window. About then, our driver hit a speed bump too fast and my head was thrown painfully into a bump in the ceiling. I wanted to strangle someone!

Shikara Boats provided transport to the houseboats, which used to be filled with tourists but which were nearly empty in July, 2005

Soon, we were driving through some of the downtown streets of Srinagar. A lot of old memories were coming back to me. One striking difference now was that armed soldiers were placed about every one hundred feet on all the major streets and avenues. Like at the airport, they all wore helmets and flack jackets and had automatic rifles. Also, at various locations there were fortified gun emplacements, with sand bags and soldiers. And barbed wire was used in many places.

There was definitely a sense of tension and danger in the environment. I was glad we would only be there a couple days. In fact, I could already sense the relief we would all feel when we departed.

Before long, we arrived at the area called "The Bund." That's an avenue which is beside one shore of Dal Lake. Several of the mountains loom nearby.

We crawled out of the cramped mini-van and unloaded our baggage. The Bund is also the docking area where many of the small boats take on passengers going to houseboats.

On Dal Lake there are literally hundreds of large, luxurious houseboats which serve as hotels for visitors. Legend has it that hundreds of years ago, private ownership of land was restricted. To circumvent that, wealthy people had houseboats built.

We boarded two small, colorful boats with their "shikaras,"or oarsmen. The boats have a streamlined shape, a canopy for shade and comfortable cushions. The boatmen have distinctive paddles which have a heart-shape at the end, in the unique Hebrew-style. We leisurely covered a distance of about three hundred meters or so across the lake, and we arrived at our houseboat: "The New Moon." It was docked beside: "The Garden of Heaven."

A RE-INTERVIEW WITH AZIZ KASHMIRI

After getting unloaded, I used Dnyanesh's cell phone and called Aziz Kashmiri, author of the book *Christ in Kashmir*. The time was about five p.m., and it was sunny. It seemed that a lot of daylight was still left. Aziz said we were welcome to come over right away to his house. I said to Paul: "Why don't we make hay while the sun shines?" In other words, why not use our time productively and get the interview done? He and Anil agreed and we all headed off to conduct the interview.

As we got out of the taxi and then bid it goodbye in Aziz Kashmiri's neighborhood, no sooner did we approach the front door than we realized that our video camera, in its metal case, had been left in the rear part of the taxi van!

This caused a panic for us.

The taxi had driven off and we were in Aziz Kashmiri's Muslim neighborhood, potentially a hostile neighborhood for two Americans to be walking around, and we were without any way to film the interview. We made a cell phone call and a quick trip to the home of the taxi owner and fortunately recovered it safely. The taxi driver had not even yet noticed that we'd left it behind.

We arrived back at the home of Aziz Kashmiri without further incident, and he was waiting on the porch to greet us. He embraced me warmly, and he welcomed us all into his home.

We set up the camera on the tripod in the living room and had a wonderful interview. His son, who is now the editor of *The Roshni (The Light)* newspaper, was there along with several of his grandchildren. They brought hot tea and cookies for us during the interview.

Aziz Kashmiri and one of his associates, Professor Fida Hassnain, are considered the luminaries of the field of Jesus in India research related to evidence and relics in Kashmir. Between the two of them, they have compiled masses of data. Aziz Kashmiri has done an immense amount of work establishing the Jewish origins of people in Kashmir, going back to before the time of Christ. There are distinct parallels in language to Hebrew, as well as customs. It is difficult to find anyone with as much conviction as Aziz Kashmiri on the likelihood of Jesus having survived the crucifixion and then having returned to India.

The interview reviewed many of the central points that are made in **Christ in Kashmir**. Azis Kashmiri has become convinced beyond doubt that Jesus of Nazareth actually survived the crucifixion and later returned to Srinagar, Kashmir, and that the historical Jesus – the Jesus beyond myth and legend and beyond human exaggeration, beyond the manipulation and distortion of Biblical stories written a century or more after his life – that the real Jesus really is buried there. He is convinced that Christianity took a wrong turn with the mythological story that Jesus died on the cross, was resurrected to life after three days and later ascended to heaven to sit at the right hand of God, Jesus' father. He believes that to build a religious structure, a human belief system, Christianity effectively closed the door to any knowledge or consideration of the latter part of Jesus' life on earth and his eventual burial as a prophet among the Jewish population of Kashmir. He believes that the latter part of Jesus' life, after Jesus' execution by the Romans was not completed, is factual with a chain of historical evidence that the western world has quite deliberately blinded itself to seeing. Virtually any member of the sect known as the Ahmadiyya Muslims would believe and express this point of view.

Aziz Kashmiri provided us with a warning. The tomb of Yuz Asaf would not be as accessible to us now as it was during my first visit a couple decades before. There had been a great deal of conflict in the neighborhood. Outsiders were not welcomed. They were shunned. The tomb was locked up, to prevent entrance or filming inside.

We were warned that there could be a furor in the neighborhood if they even saw a film crew show up with camera equipment. The Muslim community near the Rozabal tomb was taking a firm stand against intrusion by outsiders. Furthermore, the mainstream branches of Islam persecuted the Ahmadiyyas who revered the tomb as the tomb of Christ.

Things had become so bad that the Ahmadiyya Muslims had essentially been excommunicated. They were not even allowed now to make pilgrimage to Mecca, which is required of all true Muslims as one of the tenants of the religion, for them to accomplish during their lifetime.

Aziz Kashmiri felt it might be impossible for us to film at the tomb at all.

He mentioned that a BBC filming team had also visited him in the last couple of years. They also had done an interview with him and made inquiry about the significance of the Rozabal tomb. Something about the controversy had been broadcast in Great Britain, but it had never reached the United States, where nobody seemed to know anything about this question.

At the end, around sunset, we made our farewells, bought some extra copies of his book and departed.

Aziz Kashmiri and his grandson

On the way out, I noticed that on his bookshelf there was a copy of the first book I had written. I felt honored to find ***King of Travelers: Jesus' Lost Years in India*** among the books of his library. I was indeed delighted to see Aziz Kashmiri again!

It was the fact that I had mentioned his book, in an article I wrote for the Lampasas newspaper, that caused me to face complete rejection in my fundamentalist Christian hometown of Lampasas, Texas. No one in Lampasas had ever read Aziz Kashmiri's book or even seen a copy of it. They had no idea what was in it. The mere fact that I had mentioned in print the name of a book called ***Christ in Kashmir*** was enough to get me blackballed!

THE TOMB OF YUZ ASAF

For those who have read my book ***King of Travelers: Jesus' Lost Years in India*** or who have seen the film **"Jesus in India,"** this may be unnecessary repetition. However, I think a reference to how I first became embroiled in the mystery of the Rozabal Tomb may be helpful, nevertheless.

The purported tomb of Jesus' mother Mary in Murree,
Pakistan, the town that was named after her but mis-spelled

Briefly put: a Pakistani Christian bartender told me that a Pakistani beer, Murree Beer, is named after the burial place of Mary, the mother of Jesus. He further explained that some people believe that Jesus survived the crucifixion in a state of near-death, was assisted to escape the tomb by a back tunnel entrance and recuperated later in Damascus. After that, he returned to India with a caravan, returning to the land where he had spent much of his youth. His mother Mary and others accompanied him on the journey. Mary became very ill and died at the place named after her, Murree, in northern Pakistan.

According to the continuing story, as I first heard it from the Pakistani Christian bartender, Jesus continued eastward to Kashmir, became a spiritual adviser to King Shalivahan and settled down there. He married at about forty-five, had several children, and he lived to about one hundred and ten. He was buried in Srinagar at Rozabal. The purported tomb of Mother Mary, today, is behind barbed wire and beneath a television tower, both of which serve to protect it from intruders and vandals.

I heard this same story again, exactly, from Aziz Kashmiri in the autumn of 1974 on my first trip to India! I was in Srinagar, staying at a houseboat on the Jhellum River. I had gone to a local bookstore and very much by chance or accident had found Aziz Kashmiri's book: *Christ in Kashmir*. But there are no "accidents," are there?

I had met with him at his newspaper office and interviewed him for two hours or longer. He had finally told me that I could visit the tomb myself, if I wished. Yes, I wished!

The taxi driver had dropped me off at the tomb of Yuz Asaf late in the afternoon. The mountains of the Kashmir valley are high, and the sun had dropped below the summits.

At that moment back in 1974, everything was so peaceful. The lighting was subdued, and several children played with a ball in an open area, near the tomb. An elderly man, the caretaker, welcomed me just outside the tomb. I removed my boots and socks, and entered the building. An intricately carved, wooden sarcophagus enclosed a simple, white stone tomb.

I had kneeled and prayed to Lord Jesus. What if, against all odds, this was all true? What if I, at that moment, happened to be the only Christian on planet Earth praying at the true resting place of Jesus? Had there been an unbelievable sequence of coincidences which had brought me there, or was everything in divine order? That's what had

Anil speaks to a local Muslim about the tomb of
Yuz Asaf that is inside the enclosure in the background

gone through my mind about three decades before while at that ancient, mysterious tomb.

Now, in 2005, our Indian team readied all their equipment and set off on the boat with their shikara. A driver with an SUV would take them to the tomb of Yuz Asaf. We wished them all Godspeed and good fortune and safe passage! We knew that potentially they were risking their lives.

Paul and I looked at each other and let out a deep breath. It was one of those times when Paul and I had to have faith and turn everything over to divine order. We were on pins and needles! But we convinced ourselves that our Indian team was very capable and everything would be okay. At least we thought we knew that.

A LABYRINTH OF CHANNELS

Paul and I asked our trustworthy shikara boatman, who worked for our houseboat, if he could take us for a late afternoon ride. He was delighted to do so and took us for a very pleasant little outing. We thought it would be a safe and relaxing way for us to pass the nervous hours until Anil and the rest of the team returned.

The air was cool and fragrant with the smell of blossoms as our boat glided along Dal Lake. I had brought my trusty Nikon binoculars along, as well as my Nikon FM camera. I handed Paul the binoculars as he looked at some of the dozens of distant houseboats.

Each houseboat had its own distinctive name written on a sign across the top of the entrance area. Such as: "London Soho Club," "City of Chicago," "The Golden Rose" and so on. Paul was reading off the names one by one. As he looked through the binoculars, continuing to read the names aloud, he read off "Young Republicans for Bush" in a complete deadpan – and for a moment I took him seriously.

"What!!!" I exclaimed, "let me look!"

Paul handed me the binoculars and as I searched for the houseboat named "Young Republicans for Bush," Paul suddenly said: "Ha, just pulling your leg!"

He had me going there for a minute!

And then our thoughts returned to our team that we hoped was safely filming at the Rozabal tomb. There was certainly no way for us to communicate with them. And we had no way to know that their visit there not only brought in the police but was practically causing a riot among the Muslims who lived in that neighborhood.

Our thoughts returned to the tranquility of our surroundings on the lake. It was like a lost world, with many winding channels through thick vegetation, and the houses along the edge of the lake for people who lived there and rarely left. There were children who were paddling to school by boat. There were people who did all their shopping paddling along the lake from one store to the next. It was a world apart, a

*Those who live near the tomb of Yuz Asaf
became hostile over our intrusion and filming*

world unto itself. Who could imagine that armed conflict was going on less than a few miles away?

Our boatman expertly took us through a winding series of channels, among wonderful vegetation, including some beautiful water lilies. We passed by numerous secluded houseboats and many shops and other businesses which cater only to water-borne customers. The Himalayan peaks which rim the valley on all sides were always visible. Also, often in sight, there was an ancient fortress which was atop a hill within the valley. We only heard bird calls and water sounds as we glided around.

I told Paul that on my first trip to Kashmir, I went on such a boat ride and found a store selling woolens. In particular, beautiful shawls for ladies. I bought one for my mother which was of very soft, white wool with gorgeous embroideries of flowers. When you turned the shawl over, the flower colors were different on the other side. It was called a "magic shawl." It became one of my mother's favorite possessions; she wore it often.

Our affable boatman was listening and smiling.

"Do you know of such a shop?" I asked.

"Yes," he replied, "just up ahead, in five minutes or so."

He paddled us up to the floating shop, and we removed our footwear at the entrance. My goodness, I thought, it may have been the same shop I visited years ago!

The oars of the Shikara boatmen were heart-shaped,
just like the oars used by ancient Israelis

It was!

Electrical wiring was connected to the shop, so it had an electric fan and even a refrigerator. The owner could also accept credit cards!

The owner and his helper gave Paul and me cold Pepsis in bottles, with drinking straws. And a tray of cookies. And yes, even two packages of Lay's Potato Chips.

We sat on cushions on the wonderfully carpeted floor. Some of the Kashmiri carpets show one color from one side, such as blue, and the same carpet, viewed from the other side may be green! That was very unusual indeed.

Paul made some excellent choices for his wife and daughter, and I bought one of the magic shawls for a lady friend of mine, back in Texas. We returned back to the houseboat as darkness fell.

And then, to our great relief, our team returned in high spirits!

We were told that the filming at the tomb of Yuz Asaf went well after a difficult beginning. As we had been warned, the entance to the tomb was locked. However, one of the locals (for a price) assisted our team in gaining entrance. They were able to film for about five minutes before the sound of gathering bystanders led them to stop.

The interior of the tomb had been grossly changed from the way it used to be. It was changed to give it a very Muslim appearance, with green and pink colors. All signs of the Jewish-Israeli blue were gone, and so was the ancient, delicately carved wooden structure, with all kinds of fancy flourishes, that had surrounded the sarcophagus for centuries.

Upon their exit from the tomb, a hostile crowd began to gather. The incident could have mushroomed into something with grave repercussions. However, as Anil Urmil spoke to the policeman, they hit upon the fact that they had something in common, something about a soccer team in Goa. Their lively conversation about sports, and teams they both knew, suddenly defused the situation, although the mob that soon surrounded our crew did become furious.

The fury was not just over the intrusion but over the questions that Anil and our team asked. The Muslims told Anil about a western woman who had come there once trying to obtain a DNA sample from the bones of the prophet. Supposedly, that was why the tomb was now locked up.

Months later, as Paul and Anil were editing the film, Paul came to realize that the western woman who had been mentioned was Suzanne Olsson, an author living in Florida. His contact with Ms. Olsson resulted in obtaining an interview, which was eventually intercut with the conversation our crew had with the hostile mob at the Rozabal.

In our film, as it was all cut together, it went as follows. This is a verbatim transcript:

EDWARD T. MARTIN:

For safety reasons the decision was made that Paul Davids and I would remain at the houseboat on Dal Lake where we were staying, and that Anil and the rest of our Indian team, would go over to the Tomb of Yuz Asaf, and even they had problems about security. About every 100 feet there would be an Indian soldier with an automatic rifle on duty with the flak jacket and helmet, and those soldiers were guarding against any kind of terrorism, any kind of trouble that might take place, because there was a lot of hostility and tension.

INDIA SECURITY ADVISOR:

(who is seen only in silhouette):

Getting to that particular place itself is very, very risky. And all the more due to the presence of a mosque nearby which generally has seen many gun battles between the outlaws as well as the security forces.

EDWARD T. MARTIN:

We were trying to keep it secret that there were any Americans anywhere around there, but word spread fast. They seemed to think that we might want to buy a quality Kashmiri carpet. And then as our Indian team got closer to the tomb of Yuz Asaf, they found themselves in a heavily Muslim neighborhood, and it was a very tense kind of environment.

We see local Muslims and some of our film crew near the tomb of Yuz Asaf as Suzanne Olsson speaks.

SUZANNE OLSSON:

Some time ago, the locals opened that tomb and they basically raided it, and a lot of the documents and scrolls and important things that were in there associated with this tomb have disappeared or are being held in private homes.

What they have done is rip out all the wood carvings. They removed the sarcophagus that contained all the relics, they replaced it with four glass walls, so that now it looks like a shopping mall, and they put a flimsy, fake sarcophagus inside. They painted the whole thing green, because that's the color of Islam, and they removed all traces of the blue.

Anil Kumar Urmil is present at the tomb of Yuz Asaf, also known as the Rozabal (Prophet's tomb) in a Muslim district of Srinagar.

ANIL URMIL:
In your opinion, how old is this grave?

MUSLIM BYSTANDER #1:
This is very, very ancient — we cannot say for sure how old. Our ancestors said that throughout the entire world, this grave is unique! This is a Messenger of God!! He came here from Egypt and liked the climate. He meditated here and settled here! He liked the love and hospitality of the local Muslims here. He didn't return where He came from, because He was respected here. He died here and is buried here. Those are the facts, and that's it.

PAUL DAVIDS:
(off-screen to Arif Khan):
So when Muslims living near the tomb insist that this is a prophet from Egypt, that could still mean Jesus to them?

ARIF KHAN:
In fact it corroborates the story rather than detracts from it.

(Note: The boy Jesus was taken by Joseph and Mary to Egypt to escape the threat of King Herod in Israel, and so Muslims would naturally refer to Jesus, or Yuz Asaf, as being from Egypt and would naturally avoid any reference to the fact that he was from Israel.)

EDWARD T. MARTIN:
The tomb of Yuz Asaf is hundreds of years older than the beginning of Islam. In the Muslim tradition, an enclosure building is never built around a tomb, but this tomb of Yuz

Asaf has an enclosure building around the sarcophagus, around the grave. And that is an ancient building.

A policeman shows up, speaking with Anil in Hindi, and their conversation is translated in subtitles. There is concern among the crew about the filming at the tomb, but the officer does not bring that up. The crowd of hostile bystanders grows larger.

MUSLIM BYSTANDER #2:
I am with the Jammu and Kashmir Police.

ANIL URMIL:
Oh, very good to meet you. We would like to know whose tomb this is.

MUSLIM BYSTANDER #2:
This is the tomb of a Muslim.

ANIL URMIL:
But we've heard that this is the actual tomb of Jesus Christ.

MUSLIM BYSTANDER #2:
No no no, this is not true. That's just something somebody wrote in a book. This is not the tomb of Prophet Jesus. This is the tomb of Prophet Youza.

(Note: There is no "Prophet Youza" in Islam, and the Rozabal does mean "Tomb of the Prophet." The prophets in Islam are Abraham, Jesus and Mohammed.)

ARIF KHAN:
The direction of the tomb is in the Jewish direction, east-west facing, which suggests that the inhabitant of that tomb would be a follower of Moses, would be of Israelite origin, because this was the direction they buried their dead in.

RABBI ADLERSTEIN:
There clearly were groups that did believe in aligning graves in an east-west manner rather than north-south. For many, many hundreds of years, Jews were looking along that east-

west axis. It was that band of the earth's circumference that
Jews occupied rather than largely to the north or south.

EDWARD T. MARTIN:

In the valley of Kashmir, the Temple of Solomon contained
an ancient stone inscription going back to 54 A.D. The inscription said that Yuz Asaf proclaimed his prophethood,
and that he was Yuzu, prophet of the children of Israel. In
modern times the inscription was destroyed, but not before
photographs were taken of it. And that should settle the
question whether Yuz Asaf was from Israel or Egypt.
  (Ed now reads from a source in Persian)
"DareenWacht"….Wacht means "time" in Persian….
Dareen Wacht…. At this time…..Yuz Asaf…..Jesus the
Gatherer…..(he reads more Persian words)… that he proclaimed his prophethood. And the other part: He was
Yuzu, prophet of the children of Israel. *(reads it in Persian)*.

SUZANNE OLSSON:

When I was given permission to get the DNA, the local
men had access to the underground tomb. Under the main
room is a cellar, and there's another tomb down there, so
it's a big room, you can walk around, there's headroom…

*(Anil then speaks with Muslim Bystander #3, who is furious that the
film crew has come there)*

ANIL URMIL:

There is a man here named Aziz Kashmiri who wrote a
book on this.

MUSLIM BYSTANDER #3:
ALL THAT IS LIES! ALL THAT IS LIES!!

ANIL URMIL:

What is your opinion? Why did he make up this story?

MUSLIM BYSTANDER #3:

Just to make a quick buck — why else?

SUZANNE OLSSON:

Someone in Kashmir told me, who had been down there many many years before all this militancy, before the tomb was altered, and they said that Yuz Asaf isn't in the ground. Behind one of those stone walls is a ledge. And they put him on that ledge and sealed it off, so there is a false wall, and He is behind that false wall.

MUSLIM BYSTANDER #1:

This is becoming an INSULT to the Holy Quran! So if someone says that Jesus Christ is buried here this is an insult both to Muslims and to our Holy Quran! This the Muslims will not tolerate! That is why the government agreed to lock this place up!

SUZANNE OLSSON:

They had said at the time, we're only going to be removing rocks from where the feet are, so that you have access to the feet, we don't want to remove the whole wall. So they've seen it, they know there's a body there. Yes, DNA can be recovered – if there's bones, they can get the DNA.

(Note: the people assisting Suzanne Olsson at that time had a specific reason to want her to see the bones of the feet.)

MAN INTERVIEWING SUZANNE:

It doesn't matter how old the bones are?

SUZANNE OLSSON:

No, we have 4,000 year old – or 5,000 year old Tocharian mummies that they're getting DNA from regularly.

MUSLIM BYSTANDER #1:

(referring to Suzanne Olsson)

A western lady came here to dig up the grave to get DNA samples. That's why this place is locked up, because it would be an insult!

SUZANNE OLSSON:

I received all the approvals I needed, but at the last minute there was some militancy, and this was shortly after 9/11, and the project collapsed.

ED MARTIN:

One of the significant aspects of the tomb of Yuz Asaf is a carving of two stone feet. The stone feet have strange marks, as though at the time of the burial, the artist was trying to show that that individual had undergone a crucifixion, and to preserve that knowledge in stone. And of course the Muslim caretakers now keep it covered over with a cloth, because they do not want attention to be drawn to that fact.

At Rozabal Tomb, a carving of the feet of prophet "Yuz Asaf"
shows crucifixion scars and sacrament candles placed around the feet

HEMIS MONASTERY IN LADAKH

As I mentioned earlier, it was our intention to fly from Srinagar to Ladakh, to visit the Hemis Monastery, which is at an elevation of 14,000 feet. We had plane tickets to go there, but the night before our departure from Srinagar, we heard from the Tibetan Buddhist restaurant owner who had been trying to protect us, that the chief minister of Kashmir was booked onto the same plane as our film crew. Not only that, but many of his ministers were to fly on the plane too. The chief minister had been targeted for numerous assassination attempts. The report was that there had been ten attempts, and in one incident, one of his relatives had been abducted.

Suddenly our fears were greatly magnified. Especially when we discovered it was common knowledge that he was going to be on our plane. One shoulder-harnessed heat-seeking missile could take down the plane and that would be the end of us – and this film! We saw the threat as a real possibility, and so we canceled our tickets for that plane.

The problem was that we hadn't investigated what our alternatives were. Our tickets were not transferable to another flight. There would be no other flight to Ladakh out of Srinagar for a week, and even that one might have been fully booked. Furthermore, we had come to Kashmir intending only to stay one or two days at most, and we hadn't brought money with us to purchase other airplane tickets with cash. In fact, we didn't even have enough cash left to pay for another night in the houseboat.

Upon arriving at the airport, and after going through four levels of security in which our bags were fully searched every time (and we were even forced to dispose of camera batteries), we learned that we could not buy other plane tickets with an American Express card. It was not recognized there. We might have been able to buy tickets with a VISA card, but it was a Sunday and no one in the VISA office was answering the phone. Our VISA cards for some reason were not working, the numbers weren't being recognized.

On top of all of this, with the level of security in the airport, the guards demanded to see our "valid" airplane tickets at once or they were going to make us leave the airport. We had nowhere to go, and wandering around the war-torn and dangerous city was not our preference, to be sure.

The tension was severe. We became heated with one another. For the first time since arriving in India, we all found ourselves at one another's throats. Who was to blame? What were we going to do?

"Ed and Paul, we told you that you never should have come here to Srinagar. You knew the risks. Even your own State department has Srinagar on the advisory not to visit because of the military dangers."

Those were the sorts of things the other crew members said to us in that heated moment of worry and near-panic.

Finally a phone call was placed to Sanjay Shetye, who had already returned to Goa. Sanjay saved us that day. Though it was Sunday, he convinced a banker friend to open his bank and wire money to us.

We waited for that money to arrive with a sense of desperation. The last plane out that had seats was about to leave. The boarding was going to close in ten minutes.

At last, with absolutely no minutes to spare, the funds arrived. We were the last ones aboard the airplane.

Divine order seemed to have protected us once again. We made it back to Delhi.

I was in despair and bitterly disappointed over our failure to go to Hemis Monastery at that time. My primary goal of all on the journey was to arrive there and spend several days attempting to gain the confidence of the monks, and then to try to convince them to reveal to us the secret of the ancient manuscript Nicolas Notovitch had seen there in 1887. However, I now believe the delay turned out for the best. We would have been going to Hemis then with no preparation. What was the likelihood, really, that we would have obtained any cooperation, showing up as visitors to the monastery, entirely unexpected?

We had a delay, but the delay enabled us to lay the groundwork for getting the interviews and footage Paul would need in order to complete the film. In his detailed "Afterword" that follows, Paul has given an account not only of how we acquired the best information available at the time, and how we accomplished the footage at Hemis at a later date, with much more help from Sanjay Shetye, Dnyanesh Moghe (who handled the Hemis photography) and even the Tibetan Buddhist restaurant owner who had aided us in Kashmir in our hours of danger. Dnyanesh even accomplished more than we ever could have hoped, when he also went to the home of the late Nicholas Roerich in Manali, India and filmed additional footage and Roerich paintings at the museum there. That was the home where Roerich's son had spent many days as the husband of the very famous Indian actress, Devika Rani. Why, the place had as many legends surrounding it as Pickfair in Beverly Hills had about the days of Mary Pickford and Douglas Fairbanks. We would have attempted that trip during our days in India in July, but the road had been completely washed out by monsoons; it was impassable at that time.

The point was, that although our journey to India in the summer of 2005 was nearing an end, probably the most difficult parts of the creation of the film **"Jesus in India"** were just beginning.

IN NEW DELHI AGAIN

Paul and Anil were determined to return to Goa for a few days before they had to return to Los Angeles. Instead of going to Goa, I had other plans. Therefore, back in New Delhi, we all said our farewells and went our separate ways. I gave Binny a hug and a financial offering. I also gave a financial offering to Rajneesh. I thanked Anil for all of his hard work and thanked everyone else, also. I left Rajneesh's apartment and put my luggage into a taxi van with a driver. We headed to the Hotel Millennium 2000 DX on Dariba Pan, near the New Delhi Railway Station. This was the place where Paul and I took refuge before from the heat wave.

In the next few days, I spent some time at the Ashoka Ashram at Mehrauli, which is in the south part of Delhi. I was waiting for my departure plane flight on Aeroflot, scheduled for late July. I went for an elephant ride one afternoon in the bazaar area near the train station. She was a sweetheart! I also spent some pleasant time at Connaught Circus, a shopping area in central Delhi. The "circus," I think, refers to the circular shape of its configuration. I also found some good bookstores.

The highest aspiration which I hope and pray for the film, **"Jesus in India,"** is that everyone who sees it will be helped on his or her unique spiritual path. And that everyone will be encouraged to be more tolerant and flexible toward the spiritual beliefs of other people. And also, I would hope that everyone gets a positive boost and a good dose of optimism and entertainment! I hope the controversy will not be too overwhelming for too many people. God gave us brains so we would use them. We've tried to use ours. And like Binny and myself, honest people looking at the same set of data can come to opposite conclusions, for different reasons.

Personally, I plan to do more research in the future, God willing, returning to India and elsewhere. I plan to search for more evidence about the lost years in the life of Jesus. Perhaps unknown copies of ancient documents will surface. Perhaps new, unexpected DNA evidence will bring startling results. I think that much more in the nature of such discoveries awaits me in the future.

Before closing and turning the ending of this book over to Paul
Davids for his "Afterword," I would like to quote a passage from
Swami Abhedananda's classic 1922 book, ***Journey into Kashmir
and Tibet***. You'll find that he spells the Hemis Monastery as 'Himis'
– it has often been spelled both ways. It is also referred to as Hemis
Gompa or Himis Gompa, in that Gompa means monastery in Tibetan:

"Several years ago a Russian traveler, Nicolas Notovitch by name,
came on a visit to Tibet. He fell from a hill near Himis monastery and
broke one of his legs. Local people brought him to the rest house of
the monastery. The lamas nursed him for a month and a half and re-
stored him to normalcy. He came to learn from one of the lamas that
Jesus Christ had been to India according to the records in a manuscript preserved in the library of the monastery. He had the manuscript brought to him and got it translated into Russian. On his return
to his native land he wrote a book entitled '***The Unknown Life of
Jesus Christ***.' In this book he discussed thoroughly the matter of
Christ's sojourn in India. While in America the Swami (Abhedananda)
had gone through the book and felt deeply interested in its subject. As
a matter of fact he had taken so much trouble in coming all the way to
the monastery of Himis to check up the truth of what he had read. He
now made enquiries with the lamas and came to know that it was true.
Then he requested to be allowed to see the book containing this information.

"The lama who was acting as our guide took a manuscript from
the shelf and showed it to the Swami. He said that it was an exact
translation of the original manuscript which was lying in the monastery of Marbour near Lhasa. The original manuscript is in Pali, while
the manuscript preserved in Himis is in Tibetan. It consists of fourteen chapters and two hundred twenty-four couplets (slokas). The
Swami got some portion of the manuscript translated with the help of
the lama attending on him.

"Below are given the activities of Jesus Christ in India according
to this manuscript."(End of quotation from Abhedananda's book.

The following are some key passages of the manuscript which I
quote directly from the translation in Nicolas Notovitch's 1894 book
The Unknown Life of Jesus Christ. Once again, the ancient
manuscript itself is entitled: ***The Life of Saint Issa, the Best of
the Sons of Men***. I quoted this also in my first book, ***King of
Travelers: Jesus' Lost Years in India***. The point is, if this

chapter about Kashmir and the Tomb of Yuz Asaf has left you in a quandary, wondering how it could possibly be as the Ahmadiyya Muslims claim (that it is actually the tomb of Jesus Christ) then consider the following account carefully. It fills in the details of Jesus' Missing Years between the ages of twelve and thirty, when he began his ministry in Judea. If we could ever obtain the manuscript that Nicolas Notovitch and Swami Abhedananda examined – if it would suddenly "appear" at the Hemis Monastery or elsewhere – we could begin the scientific tests that could tell us if it is an ancient account dating to the time of Christ, and possibly a true account. Unfortunately, we do not know the truth yet. And if the document is being deliberately withheld from public release, we do not know who is withholding it or why, or on whose directive.

Here is the excerpt from the purportedly ancient manuscript. I take the liberty of jumping forward in the text for the purpose of citing what I feel to be some of the most significant stanzas:

I

1.   The earth has trembled and the heavens have wept, because of the great crime just commited in the land of Israel.

2.   For they have put to torture and executed the great just Issa, in whom dwelt the spirit of the world.

3.   Which was incarnated in a simple mortal, that men might be benefited and evil thoughts exterminated thereby.

4.   And that it might bring back to a life of peace, of love and happiness, man degraded by sin, and recall to him the only and indivisible Creator whose mercy is boundless and infinite.

5.   This is what is related on this subject by the merchants who have come from Israel.

IV

1.   And now the time had come, which the Supreme Judge, in his boundless clemency, had chosen to incarnate himself in a human being.

2.   And the Eternal Spirit, which dwelt in a state of complete inertness and supreme beatitude, awakened and detached itself from the Eternal Being for an indefinite period.

3.   In order to indicate, in assuming the human form, the means of identifying ourselves with the Divinity and of attaining eternal felicity.

4.   And to teach us, by his example, how we may reach a state of moral purity and separate the soul from its gross envelope, that it may attain the perfection necessary to enter the Kingdom of Heaven which is immutable and where eternal happiness reigns.

5.   Soon after, a wonderful child was born in the land of Israel; God himself, through the mouth of this child, spoke of the nothingness of the body and of the grandeur of the soul.

6.   The parents of this new-born child were poor people, belonging by birth to a family of exalted piety, which disregarded its former worldly greatness to magnify the name of the Creator and thank him for the misfortunes with which he was pleased to try them.

7.   To reward them for their perseverance in the path of truth, God blessed the first-born of this family; he chose him as his elect, and sent him forth to raise those that had fallen into evil, and to heal them that suffered.

8.   The divine child, given the name of Issa, commenced even in his most tender years to speak of the one and indivisible God, exhorting the people that had strayed from the path of righteousness to repent and purify themselves of the sins they had committed.

9.   People came from all parts to listen and marvel at the words of wisdom that fell from his infant lips; all the Israelites united in proclaiming that the Eternal Spirit dwelt within this child.

10. When Issa had attained the age of thirteen, when an Israelite should take a wife,

11. The house in which his parents dwelt and did earn their livelihood in modest labor became a meeting place for the rich and noble, who desired to gain for a son-in-law the young Issa, already celebrated for his edifying discourses in the name of the Almighty

12. It was then that Issa clandestinely left his father's house, went out of Jerusalem, and, in company with some merchants, traveled toward Sind.

13. That he might perfect himself in the divine word and study the laws of the great Buddhas.

V

1. In the course of his fourteenth year, young Issa, blessed by God, journeyed beyond the Sind and settled among the Aryans in the beloved country of God.

2. The fame of his name spread along the Northern Sindh. When he passed he passed through the country of the five rivers and the Radjipoutan, the worshippers of the God Djaine begged him to remain in their midst.

3. But he left the misguided admirers of Djaine and visited-Juggernaut, in the province of Orsis, where the remains of Viassa-Krishna rest, and where he received a joyous welcome from the white priests of Brahma.

4. They taught him to read and understand the Vedas, to heal by prayer, to teach and explain the Holy Scripture, to cast out evil spirits from the body of man and give him back human semblance.

5. He spent six years in Juggernaut, Rajegriha, Benares, and the other holy cities; all loved him, for Issa lived in peace with the Vaisyas and the Soudras, to whom he taught the Holy Scripture.

6. But the Brahmans and the Kshatriyas declared the Great Para-Brahma forbade them to approach those whom he had created from his entrails and from his feet.

7. That the Vaisyas were authorized to listen only to the reading of the Vedas, and that never save on feast days.

8. That the Soudras were not only forbidden to attend the reading of the Vedas, but to gaze upon them even, for their condition was to perpetually serve and act as slaves to the Brahmans, the Kshatriyas, and even to the Vaisyas.

9. "Death alone can free them from servitude," said Para-Brahma. "Leave them, therefore, and worship with us the gods who will show their anger against you if you disobey them."

10. But Issa would not heed them; and going to the Soudras, preached against the Brahmans and the Kshatriyas.

11. He strongly denounced the men who robbed their fellow-beings of their rights as men saying: "God the Father establishes no difference between his children, who are all equally dear to him."

12. Issa denied the divine origin of the Vedas and the Pouranas, declaring to his followers that one law had been given to men to guide them in their actions.

13. "Fear thy God, bow down the knee before Him only, and to Him only must thy offerings be made."

14. Issa denied the Trimourti and the incarnation of Para-Brahma in Vishnou, Siva, and other gods, saying:

15. "The Eternal Judge, the Eternal Spirit, composes the one and indivisible soul of the universe, which alone creates, contains, and animates the whole."

16. "He alone has willed and created, he alone has existed from eternity and will exist without end; he has no equal neither in the heavens nor on this earth."

17. "The Great Creator shares his power with no one, still less with inanimate objects as you have been taught, for he alone possesses supreme power."

18. "He willed it, and the world appeared; by one divine thought, he united the waters and separated them from the dry portion of the globe. He is the cause of the mysterious life of man, in whom he has breathed a part of his being."

VI

1. The white priests and the warriors becoming cognizant of the discourse addressed by Issa to the Soudras, resolved upon his death and sent their servants for this purpose in search of the young prophet.

2. But Issa, warned of this danger by the Soudras, fled in the night from Juggernaut, gained the mountains, and took refuge in the Gothamide Country, the birthplace of the great Buddha Sakya-Mouni, among the people who admired the only and sublime Brahma.

3. Having perfectly learned the Pali tongue, the just Issa applied himself to the study of the sacred rolls of Soutras.

4. Six years later, Issa, whom the Buddha had chosen to spread his holy word, could perfectly explain the sacred rolls.

5. He then left Nepal and the Himalayan Mountains, descended into the valley of Rajipoutan and went westward, preaching to diverse people of the supreme perfection of man,

6. And of the good we must do unto others, which is the surest means of quickly merging ourselves in the Eternal Spirit. "He who shall have recovered his primitive purity at death," said Issa, "shall have obtained the forgiveness of his sins, and shall have the right to contemplate the majestic figure of God."

VII

1. The words of Issa spread among the pagans, in the countries through which he traveled, and the inhabitants abandoned their idols.

IX

1.   Issa, whom the Creator had chosen to recall the true God to the people that were plunged in depravities, was twenty-nine years of age when he arrived in the land of Israel.

XIV

10.   And the disciples of Saint Issa left the land of Israel and went in all directions among the pagans, telling them that they must abandon their gross errors, think of the salvation of their souls, and of the perfect felicity in store for men in the enlightened and immaterial world where, in repose and in all his purity, dwells the great Creator in perfect majesty.

11.   Many pagans, their kings and soldiers, listened to these preachers, abandoned their absurd beliefs and deserted their priests and their idols to sing the praises of the all-wise Creator of the universe, the King of kings, whose heart is filled with infinite mercy.

(To read the entire text, the reader is advised to obtain a copy of *The Unknown Life of Jesus Christ* by Nicolas Notovitch.)

The tomb of Yuz Asaf in July, 2005

Photography and Videography at the tomb of Yuz Asaf
is strictly prohibited -- WHY?

13. Afterword by Paul Davids

> *"Always remember,"* said the Master, *"that no circumstance or event that ever happens to you will be as important as what you choose to think about it. That means,"* he continued, *"your thoughts about anything are either conscious choices or reactions. But either way, your thoughts are as real as a stone or piece of wood, and they have lasting consequences."*
>
> *"But what if the event is a violent action, committed unfairly against myself or another?"* asked a student. *"And what if it has life-or-death consequences? Will my thoughts about it still be more important than the event itself?"*
>
> *"All the more so!"* boomed the Master, standing up suddenly for emphasis. *"Every creature in the Creation has the right of self-defense when attacked. But if you act with hatred and revenge, you become as evil as the wrongdoer. Keep your inner balance and, whatever you do, be aware of what you are letting yourself think."*
>
> ---*folk story from the Himalayas*

What I remember most about our departure from India at the Mumbai International Airport on July 26, 2005, was the driving rain. So many times, as we had traveled throughout India, we had managed to stay a few days ahead of the monsoons as we ventured from south to north.

By the end, those monsoons had caught up with us, with a vengeance. As Anil and I sat waiting for news about whether our plane would be cleared for take-off (Ed Martin was remaining behind for a while longer), rain began drenching Mumbai in what would become one of those one hundred year storms.

We were blind to how serious it would become as the hours ticked away before take-off. At one point, we were cleared to board our plane, and then as we sat aboard for a long time, the plane was not even authorized to make its way toward the runway.

We had to get off the plane and return to the waiting area.

The roof of the airport reverberated with the drama of the early phase of a storm that would make international news before we ever landed back in Los Angeles.

The break in the storm was brief. It was not really a break, but it was a reduction in intensity – just enough so we could eventually be cleared for take-off. We had no way to know then that we would be the last airplane out of the Mumbai Airport for about one week. Or that the storm would unleash thirty-three inches of rain on Mumbai within a twenty-four hour period.

Nor could we imagine the numbers of people who would die in that storm. The deaths in Mumbai exceeded one thousand, most from electrocution. Many of the shacks in Mumbai have electrical wiring that doesn't run high above on elevated cables but instead is close to the ground. Three feet of water drowned everything that wasn't built to withstand such a flood. Electrical wires crackled from being under-water, and people making their way through puddles that had become almost a river were literally shocked to death.

By the time of our landing back home, Mumbai was everywhere in the news. By the grace of God, or by Divine Order, or however one might describe it, we had been protected from harm throughout the six week filming journey, and we had been spared from "the seeds of bad karma" right up to the very end.

Our departure from India marked the end of one phase of the making of **"Jesus in India"** and the beginning of the second part of the journey, just as challenging as our travels through India and our filming from Meenakshi in the south to the Himalayas in the north.

There was a massive amount of work ahead of me, work that would take me to locations throughout the United States, and then to Italy and also to London. There, I would continue filming with experts who could contribute to filling in the missing pieces of the puzzle that were not to be found in India.

It was also certain that part of my coming travel would take me to Texas, to be with Ed in the small town of Lampasas that had rejected him for his religious inquiry.

The work would continue to be demanding on Anil, because although he did not participate in any of the travel after India, he continued to make an important contribution. After working on a director's cut of the film for about eight months, I invited him to join me in the editing room as a fellow editor to help shape the film and complete the vision as best we could with the information that had been gleaned and the footage that had been shot.

Other colleagues would soon join me, who had not been part of the journey to India. Brian Thomas Lambert, the immensely talented composer who had created the music score for **"The Sci-Fi Boys"** came aboard to compose a fabulous, original score for **"Jesus in India."** You can hear six minutes of that score by going to www.jesus-in-india-the-movie.com – or you can order a CD of the entire musical soundtrack at the website for the film.

Bob Rotstan, Jr., who had done so much to set our film of **"Jesus in India"** in motion by having the foresight to understand the importance of the theme and its cinematic possibilities, and who had introduced me to Edward T. Martin, participated actively with many phases of post-production. He was always there when needed to critique the editing process, and he participated in each step of completion that we undertook at CCI in Burbank (California Communications, Inc.) in the comfortable and well-staffed studio on Alameda Drive, across the street from the NBC building.

I had about one hundred hours of material that had been filmed in India. It was the story of Ed leading us on a search for answers to the Biblical mystery that had haunted him since childhood. Like an artist working with paints, I had everything I needed on my pallet to paint a unique image of India and some of its people, its intense spirituality as well as its urban struggles, its ancient heritage and its vast landscapes.

What I lacked, and what I knew I would have to obtain was the input of scholars and experts who could shape the argument about the Missing Years of Jesus in a coherent way.

My style and intent was decidedly different from that of documentary filmmakers such as Michael Moore **("Fahrenheit 911," "Bowling for Columbine")** and Bill Maher (whose **"Religulous"** would not be completed for three more years).

I was not setting out to force specific conclusions on the viewer. Although Ed Martin, and those who considered themselves his allies in religious speculation, had a deep-seated conviction that Jesus of Nazareth had been to India (and that his mortal remains were buried in the Rozabal Tomb in Srinagar), I knew there were noted scholars who did not accept this theory at all. I needed to know why, and I needed another answer other than that he was resurrected from the dead and then ascended to heaven to sit at the right hand of God.

It was a debate I was seeking, but could there be a winning side in the absence of all the evidence we had been seeking?

From one point of view our mission to India had not quite ended in failure – certainly not, if only because we were able to have the Shankaracharya of Puri, one of the four ecclesiastical heads of Hinduism, go on record about Jesus in India. But we had fallen short of the success we had sought. Our planned trip to the Hemis Monastery had been canceled because of political circumstances. Our lives would have been in danger if we had proceeded at the time we had planned. It had been difficult getting Ed to accept that we would have to "lose the battle to try to win the war."

We had to plan to accomplish the mission at Hemis later. It would have to be another phase of the effort. But the search for the purportedly ancient document about Jesus in India that Russian explorer Nicolas Notovitch had translated in 1887, and which Swami Abhedananda had unambiguously confirmed in the 1920's (with further independent support from Russian artist Nicholas Roerich), would have to go on. The opportunity to pursue the Hemis Monastery part of the inquiry would not arise for several months, until nearly the end of 2005. In the meantime, there was much other production work to accomplish.

The central, pivotal contribution upon our return to Los Angeles from India came from Paramahansa Yogananda's Self-Realization Fellowship. In a way, the journey had begun at the Mother Center, atop Mount Washington about a half mile from my home, on the day Anil and I had gone to meditate there and silently ask for blessings for our journey and protection in our travels.

So I had come full circle by contacting SRF and requesting to be able to film an interview with one of the most knowledgeable monks on the subject of Jesus in India. SRF did not hesitate. They honored our efforts by granting a lengthy interview with Brother Chidananda, the head of the publications division of SRF. Brother Chidananda is responsible for the production and editorial work on all of the publications SRF undertakes of Yogananda's writings and public talks. He had recently completed work on the massive two-volume tome called ***The Second Coming of Christ: The Resurrection of the Christ Within You***.

That double-volume set of books pulled together Yogananda's writings and insights through the years about the meaning of Biblical scripture, interpreted through an understanding of Hinduism, with a focus on Jesus' message that "the Kingdom of heaven is within you." That is a principal tenant of Hinduism and is the basis of yoga, or union with the infinite through spiritual practices such as meditation and the care and conditioning of the physical body.

Was it serendipity that *The Second Coming of Christ* happened to have a chapter devoted to Yogananda's teachings about Jesus in India? Brother Chidananda had brought together all of Yogananda's writings and pronouncements and insights, inspirations and intuitions about the subject. Within those pages is to be found a summary of Christ's connection to India that begins with the three Magi who according to the *Gospel of Matthew* visited Jesus at his birth. It then continues through all the evidence from the east that Yogananda had collected supporting Jesus' travel to India between the ages of twelve and thirty.

What it does not speculate upon, because it is contrary to Yogananda's teachings (that are in so many ways a sincere blend of both Hinduism and orthodox Christianity), is whether Jesus may have survived the crucifixion and then returned to India.

Although that belief is central to the religious teachings and faith of the Ahmadiyya Muslims, who insist that Yuz Asaf and Jesus are one and the same and that the mortal remains of Jesus are in Srinagar, Yogananda was a resurrectionist. He believed literally that Jesus died and rose from the dead. His interpretation of the death and resurrection of Christ is really no different from that of the strictest Christian theologian. In fact, in a startling chapter in his *Autobiography of a Yogi*, he descrbes how his guru, Swami Sri Yukteswar, also appeared to him after death in a resurrected body. Such apparently "supernatural" occurences were not outside the structure of his philosophy at all. And that philosophy also includes brilliant and sharply intuitive talks and writings that are practical, down-to-earth, and which do not require any metaphysical belief system. He never asked anyone to believe and accept based on anyone else's pronouncements. He only asked that people practice meditation and yoga, claiming that in proper yoga practice, all the answers to the mystery of life would come in time.

Yogananda accomplished a nearly miraculous mission. He made Hindu theology not only palatable to many westerners but his life work caused thousands (maybe millions) in the west to embrace aspects of Hindu philosophy and concede the connection to Christianity. Yoga was scarcely practiced in the United States when Yogananda arrived in Boston on September 18, 1920, to be a delegate to the International Congress of Religious Liberals. By the time of Yogananda's passing in 1952, the stage was set for yoga in the west, making it inevitable that one day yoga would become as ingrained in western culture as it had always been in eastern culture.

One can easily conjecture that if Yogananda had *not* accepted the death and resurrection of Christ from the dead, as he formed Self-Realization Fellowship as the Church of All Religions, he quite likely would never have made progress in promoting international religious understanding among Christians. And that was a central goal of his mission. Yogananda embraced a rather orthodox view of Christianity and strove to show its common roots with Hinduism, and how an understanding of Hinduism's search for God within the human spirit elucidates the intended meaning of the New Testament.

As far as Jesus in Kashmir or the theory of Jesus having survived the crucifixion and living on to old age in his human body after returning to the east, those were aspects of the Jesus in India hypothesis that Yogananda never mentioned. He accepted Christianity as most Christians interpret it and built upon that acceptance to try to broaden the western perspective and bring yoga into people's lives in the west.

He did not tread where we decided to tread in the conclusion of the film **"Jesus in India."** Therefore, we especially thank SRF for its cooperation with our film, because we did examine in depth a part of Christian theology which SRF accepts as an integral part of Yogananda's teachings (i.e., Christ's death and resurrection).

Once again, our goal in the film was not to come to definitive conclusions about these most controversial issues. Our goal was, however, to permit ourselves both the courage and the audacity to seriously address these questions to try to see if another explanation of the Biblical accounts is supported by the available testimonials and evidence from long ago.

The film is therefore filled with experts who accept the reality of Christ's death and resurrection, as well as some who do not and who explain their reasons for their skepticism, and why they believe the true historical link between Jesus and India essentially has been suppressed by mainstream orthodoxy. The general lack of interest in and knowledge of St. Thomas' well-evidenced travel to India – his preaching there and dying there – is one indication of this failure on the part of western Christians to examine evidence and facts and consider implications.

The first day of filming at SRF in the library at the Mother Center was pivotal to the structure of our film. That was because Brother Chidananda took us step by step through the evidence for the reality and importance of the Notovitch document that apparently can no longer be found at Hemis Monastery. He told us about Notovitch and Swami Abhendanda and Nicholas Roerich and the Shankaracharya, and in so doing, he provided an intellectual and historical structure for the adventures and the search that we had lived in India.

He also confirmed that the previous Shankaracharya of Puri met with Sri Daya Mata (the spiritual successor to Paramahansa Yogananda) and confirmed for her that ancient documents regarding Jesus' travels in India do exist. (This was just as Professor James Deardorff had reported to Edward T. Martin in correspondence that Ed reported on in Chapter Five.) These documents were claimed to have been at the Jagannath Temple in Puri, although the previous Shankaracharya passed away before writing the book that would have chronicled some of that evidence. In **"Jesus in India,"** the current Shankaracharya claims that Jesus was in fact at the Jagannath Temple for an extended period of time, but he has not offered hope that the supporting ancient documents will be identified by the temple and made public.

SRF also graciously gave permission for me to film at the SRF Lake Shrine, located near the Pacific Ocean toward the end of Sunset

Looking up at Yogananda's personal quarters at the Self-Realization Fellowship Mother Center at Mt. Washington, Los Angeles

Boulevard. The shrine, which has an urn that contains some of the ashes of Mahatma Gandhi, is a testament to the underlying unity of the five great religions. Several views of the Lake Shrine appear toward the end of **"Jesus in India,"** including a statue of Jesus by a waterfall.

With SRF's contribution having aided the efforts greatly, my next task was to head for Texas to film Edward T. Martin on his home turf. Part of the premise of the film dealt with his personal story as someone who was strictly raised within the Church of Christ, to such an extent that his parents took him to church "every time the doors were open," he says.

He speaks of church visits three times a week. Then there came his period of questioning, his loss of certainty in all that he had been taught, and eventually he found himself ostracized because of his research about the Missing Years of Jesus and the possibility of Jesus' travels in India.

As Edward T. Martin has written, his showing an article he wrote in the local paper about his first trip to India, where he merely mentioned the existence of Aziz Kashmiri's book (***Christ in Kashmir***) caused him to be ostracized. The cold shoulder that was offered to him, by nearly everyone in his Texas hometown was a severe winter chill. He suddenly was treated almost like an unwelcome stranger among people who had known him all his life.

This indeed was part of our story. I flew to Austin, where Ed was living in the autumn of 2005. We filmed background at the State Capitol, a beautiful building. I was somewhat overwhelmed to discover how beautiful Austin is. I was unfamiliar with it. The parks were immaculate and the buildings were too. There seemed to be a pride in Austin, and I didn't even see any graffiti. The friendliness extended to the fact that we were able to walk right into the State Capitol with camera equipment, set up in the rotunda and film with a tripod, and no one objected or asked to see a permit. It was unheard of, really. The guards were simply helpful, and no questions were asked. Ed pointed out one of the large paintings in the rotunda that depicted one of his ancestors who had a key role in a battle for Texas' independence. Ed explained with pride that for a while Texas was a sovereign nation, the Republic of Texas.

Our background filming also took us to the Alamo at San Antonio, a place I had always wanted to see, as I grew up with the legends of Davy Crockett and Jim Bowie. Then we drove up to Lampasas to capture the ambiance of the small town where Ed was raised as a member of the Church of Christ.

There were at least two Churches of Christ in the town. At one of them, Preacher Elvis Fisher was kind and helpful. He remembered Ed and the conflicts that arose at one of the "other" Churches of Christ. He was open to talking about the legends of Jesus in India, but he made it clear he could find no reason to believe those legends. (He had not read Ed's book and knew nothing of the specifics of the research or the Notovitch document or St. Thomas' presence in India after the crucifixion). He discussed his belief that Jesus was in Judea during the Missing Years, being raised by Joseph and Mary as an ordinary boy ("because that's the form he took," said Elvis Fisher).

Other Church of Christ members in the predominantly fundamentalist Christian town agreed to be interviewed.

They cautioned against going anywhere "outside the Bible." They insisted that the Bible is "the Word of God." They assured me they believed "every word of it." And from those who knew Edward T. Martin "way back when" there were remarks about how different he was from the others in the town, first of all, because he liked to travel to faraway places. "It's not wrong, but it's different," I was told by one of his cousins. "It's not what other people here do." Some found fault with Ed because "he had trouble settling down." And none of them had read his book: ***King of Travelers: Jesus' Lost Years in India***. A few had picked it up and flipped through it and then put it down.

Basically, it was explained to me that the title alone was proof enough for them that it would not be a book they would be interested in. It turned out that, sometime shortly before our film was completed, Ed's one wealthy relative passed away. This particular uncle, who owned a ranch and quite a spread of cattle, had carefully avoided any conversations about Ed's book after it was first published, so as not to fester any family conflict. He had not read the book, and rather than ask Ed what it was about (he had probably heard some rumors), he spent his time with Ed asking Ed about Ed's pocket knife and how good it was for whittling. In the end, that Uncle gave the vast majority of his holdings to the Church of Christ rather than to the family, which somewhat surprised Ed who did not expect that that would be the case.

We also visited the graveyard where Ed's parents are buried, to pay our respects. In the graveyard, we came upon a statue of an angel that had been defaced, with one of its arms chopped off. I got to hear the local gossip of how it happened. There was a rivalry in town. One family against another. Smashing the arm of the angel had been somebody's "payback."

The footage we filmed in Texas, I was sure, would give the audience for the film a grasp of the local attitudes and rather narrow-minded mentality. However, there was one Texan I interviewed who owned the most famous local hamburger place, a restaurant that Elvis Presley had actually sometimes visited. Presley's photo was all over the menu, with tales about the times the "King" had wandered in for a burger while he was a soldier at nearby Fort Hood.

The owner of the hamburger place had known Ed from "way back when" and had always liked Ed, but he confided in me that there's a thin borderline between being inspired and being crazy, and he frankly couldn't say which side of the line Ed was on. He was the most open-minded interview subject I found in Texas, admitting that he was no longer "wedded" to the Church of Christ because he didn't take well to the prohibitions on dancing and beer and he didn't like the fact that gambling was forbidden too. He just couldn't imagine for a moment, however, that Jesus had survived the crucifixion. He admitted he didn't know whether Jesus had ever gone to India or not but dismissed it as rather unimportant, and he just couldn't appreciate Ed's obsession with the subject. He claimed to have read Ed's book (though there was little evidence of that in the conversation), and he summed up his position by stating that he had different views of history than Edward T. Martin.

When I was filming at SRF, I heard great praise about a Princeton professor, Prof. Elaine Pagels, who had done an enormous amount of research on the Nag Hammadi scriptures that were discovered in Egypt in the late 1940's. Those scriptures were ancient apocryphal Christian texts that included the **Gospel of Thomas**. No one had been able to date it precisely, but there was a raging debate about whether it dated back to the time of the **Gospel of Mark** (thought by most scholars to be the very first of the canonical Gospels) or whether it came along fifty or a hundred years later.

There was much talk at SRF, however, about how the **Gospel of Thomas** presented a view of Christianity that in many respects seemed closer to Hinduism than the canonical Gospels, and SRF was sure that Professor Elaine Pagels of Princeton would confirm that.

Professor Pagels had written a best seller called **Beyond Belief: The Gospel of Thomas**. I was given contact information for Prof. Pagels (who to the disappointment of SRF had never reviewed one of Yogananda's books), and SRF encouraged me to try to involve her in my film. In that I was a graduate of Princeton University, I felt that perhaps she might be responsive.

My next destination, however, was Georgetown University in Washington, DC.

Georgetown is one of the most esteemed Catholic Jesuit universities in the nation. In fact, my father was one of their few Jewish professors throughout his long career. He taught at the School of Foreign Service in Georgetown for forty years. Young Bill Clinton was one of my father's students there, and decades before that, my father had been professor to Jacqueline Kennedy. My father was a legend at Georgetown, not only as one of the founders of the School of Foreign Service, but as having assisted John F. Kennedy considerably in the conception and writing of **Profiles in Courage**, which won a Pulitzer Prize.

Thus, I had a special advantage when it came to obtaining cooperation from professors in the Department of Divinity at Georgetown.

First, Prof. Alan C. Mitchell, a former Jesuit Priest, agreed to an interview, and then Anthony Tambasco, Interim Associate Dean of the Graduate Program, also agreed. I flew to Washington in the early autumn of 2005 to conduct those interviews.

Not surprisingly, the point of view expressed was intensely Catholic. Of the two professors at Georgetown, Alan C. Mitchell showed the most flexibility of thought, and he was fully aware of the legends of Jesus having been in India. He also knew of the lore about St. Thomas in India. He was unfamiliar with the Notovitch document, however. He gave a strict interpretation of Christ's death and resurrection. He felt there was no evidence at all as to the three Magi being from India, and he even allowed that the entire story of the three Magi visiting Christ as Christ's birth may have been a sort of fable with no historic foundation.

Professor Mitchell expressed the view of the Catholic church that Jesus was in Judea throughout his youth and not in India, or at least that there was no compelling reason to believe that Jesus was in India.

Professor Tambasco stated that although the concept of Jesus having been to India might in fact be a fad or "big news" in India, he felt confident there was nothing to it, partially because no one in the religious circles he traveled in ever spoke about it. He felt it was nothing but legend. He also was not prepared to say that it was fact that St. Thomas was really in India. He was not completely persuaded by the fact that Pope John Paul II went to Chennai, India, to pay homage to St. Thomas there, or that there are branches of Thomas Christians in India who claim to have learned their Christianity directly from St. Thomas' teachings in India. He asserted that Christianity is surrounded by "legends" of the faithful, and for the most part he says the church sees no harm in this. He said that to the extent that lore and supposedly ancient relics (that are not genuine) bring people closer to the faith, they give people an emotional support and do no harm.

I never broached with him the theories that Jesus did not die on the cross and had a life afterwards. Somehow, though, I can visualize the frown he would have given to those questions.

Prof. Pagels of Princeton University came up in these conversations at Georgetown.

Prof. Mitchell and Prof. Tambasco apparently seemed to think that Prof. Pagels was much too quick to assign early dates to the apocryphal Gospels from Nag Hammadi. They were convinced that those texts were dated to a much later time period, a hundred or two hundred years following the life of Christ. Attempts to place early dates on those documents tends to intrude upon the status held by the four canonical Gospels, and Catholicism is quick to resist anything that gives special importance to the Nag Hammadi texts.

From Georgetown I took an Amtrak train up to Princeton. I called Prof. Pagels and found that she was very busy and might not be available. Also, she wasn't sure she'd be able to give me an interview, because she was recovering from a bad cold. I assured her that I would be around for almost a week and offered that perhaps I could try her after the weekend to see if she was feeling better.

In fact, when I called her Sunday night, I quickly sensed I was about to be rejected. That was when I told her that I had interviewed two professors at Georgetown, and I felt it was really a shame if she wouldn't give an interview, because I felt that she should have a chance to reply to what they said about her. That got the response I was looking for. *"What did they say about me?"* she asked. The more she heard from me, the more determined she became that I absolutely must interview her the following day.

Coincidentally, it was the one day of the semester that she was giving a lecture about the ***Gospel of Thomas***. I attended the wonderful lecture in a hall where I had heard lectures myself during my undergraduate days as a student at Princeton. Then I conducted the filmed interview in her office.

There was much that came out in that interview that was a great surprise. The largest surprise was Prof. Pagels' admission that from the standpoint of religious scholarship and history, *"we cannot rule out the possibility that Jesus traveled to India."*

This in itself was a major victory, I felt, for Edward T. Martin's mission and quest. If his theories were far off the mark or shrouded in nothing but unfounded legends and woefully unsubstantiated documents, then it would seem that Prof. Pagels would not have opened the door to the possibility. The fact that she did not close the door was in itself remarkable.

But that was not all. As she analyzed the **Gospel of Thomas** for me, there was one example after another of overlaps between the teachings of Christ, as presented in that apocryphal Gospel, and basic Hindu beliefs. There were hints of reincarnation ("Blessed is he who comes into being before he comes into being"), emphases on the divine feminine aspect of God (as in Hinduism), the importance on finding the light within oneself (as in Hindu yoga) and much more.

Prof. Pagels preferred the explanation that Jesus had encountered teachings of Hinduism and Buddhism in the Middle East. She referred to Jesus as a "village rabbi" and considered it unlikely that a "village rabbi" had traveled all the way to India. However she also claimed to be unfamiliar with the evidence: unfamiliar with Notovitch, Swami Abhendanda, Roerich, Yuz Asaf, the Rozabal Tomb in Srinagar. It was a line of scholarly inquiry outside the realm in which she had specialized. And she had no explanation for Jesus' Missing Years.

The former fundamentalist from the Texas small town, who had stood against his town and been castigated, now had a Princeton University religion scholar conceding that the cause for which he had devoted his life "could not be ruled out" as possibly being true.

I felt it was a great day and also was a step toward justifying the massive effort I myself had put into the research and the film.

From Princeton, I took the train to Amherst, Massachusetts, to interview a dear old friend, Paul R. Fleishman, M.D. Dr. Fleishman, a famous psychiatrist who had lectured at Yale and written more than half a dozen books on the "healing zones" of psychiatry and the overlap with the healing powers of religion, agreed to give an interview for my film. His knowledge of India was immense. He had traveled there numerous times and had studied every aspect of the predominant religions and culture and history.

In regard to the interview, however, his caviat was that he could not say anything specific or make any historic claims about our subject matter. As for Jesus, he could not even take the position that Jesus ever historically existed. He did not know if Jesus ever really existed or had done any of the things attributed to him by writers of the New Testament.

Apart from general observations about what Hindus and Buddhists believe, he could only offer "psychiatric" observations on what it means for someone to take on a gigantic quest that has all-consuming importance to the individual. He could not talk about Ed specifically, because he had never met him – and even if he had, it would have been unprofessional to draw any conclusions about anyone who was not a patient of his, and unethical to reveal anything about anyone who *was* a patient. This left little latitude for our interview, so far as my film was concerned.

The one remark he made that did have special importance was when he discussed Socrates, who had insisted on asking his fellow Greeks difficult questions and stating unpopular views that he believed to be correct. Whether Socrates was inspired or obsessed was a legitimate matter of debate (just as whether Ed Martin was inspired or obsessed was a legitimate question). But Socrates was willing to die for the right to ask very unpopular questions and to take unpopular positions, and in fact he DID die for it. He was forced to swallow the poison hemlock.

Ed had had a taste of that kind of medicine himself.

Dr. Fleischman and I went way back, friends since our college days. We spoke of the dream of some day experiencing India together, and we reminisced. Little of his five hour interview ended up in the film, though it would be of great value for more general subjects regarding India and why India held such a fascination for him.

When we parted ways, I went to New York, where I had a very special goal in mind. There, Daniel Entin, Director of the Nicholas Roerich Museum, granted me an interview about Jesus in India, and he had quite a lot to say.

The fabulously talented Russian artist, Nicholas Roerich, was bound into the Jesus in India research in inextricable ways. Roerich, as you know from Ed Martin's writings, traveled throughout the Himalayas on several challenging expeditions in the 1920's. He knew all about the purported finding of Nicolas Notovitch at the Hemis Monastery and had investigated the claims. I was thrilled to discover from Daniel Entin that Roerich had written reports about the claims of Jesus having been in India, and that Roerich believed it. At least, he had believed it until he was pressured, for political reasons in Russia, to retract that belief in his later years.

In 1926 Roerich confirmed the existence of the manuscript that was translated by both Notovitch and Abhendananda thirty years apart

Daniel Entin (Left), Director of the Nicholas Roerich Museum in New York, with Paul Davids

from one another. His reports ended up summarized in the *New York Sun* in 1926. They were headline stories. Jesus had studied with Buddhists in India! And Daniel Entin still had the headlines, which appear in our film.

The Roerich Museum graciously granted permission for me to film Roerich's Himalayan paintings and include them in **"Jesus in India."** This was an invaluable contribution to our effort. In fact, one of the paintings in the museum even _depicted_ Jesus in India. It is called "St. Issa and the Skull."

At that stage, I had a massive amount of interview material to intercut with our adventure in India, and Brian T. Lambert was making excellent progress in composing principal themes for the music score, even though the film was not in final edited form.

To the best of my recollection, it was around November of 2005 when my second unit cameraman, Dnyanesh Moghe (who is himself now an accomplished director of feature films in India) offered to go to the Hemis Monastery. The Tibetan restaurant owner, who had helped us and protected us during our days in Srinagar in Kashmir, contacted someone he knew who was connected with the monastery. Sanjay Shetye arranged the travel. Edward T. Martin's dream of initiating a direct questioning of the monks at the monastery was about to come true.

I prepared a comprehensive list of questions. A translator was hired to pose the questions about the missing manuscript and the supposed ancient portrait of Jesus said to exist within the monastery's archives. And that fall, at Hemis, as a second-unit effort for the film, the footage at Hemis was obtained.

With the footage in hand, I engaged two Tibetan translators in Los Angeles. The results of this effort were decidedly mixed. Once again, the door was not closed by the monks at the monastery. It was admitted that the "legend" might possibly be true and that the evidence might possibly exist at Hemis. The Dalai Lama was cited as a possible source for confirmation of the story, but once again, this was made to seem as second hand information. There was a definite awareness at Hemis of these legends. But then where was the document? What had Notovitch been shown? What had Swami Abhedananda been given to translate? Why did no one know? And why were so many ancient documents held as "untouchable" behind glass doors in cabinets that were closed with yarn tied in knots?

One of the key monks at Hemis himself cited that they had to tread carefully, because if they had such information, it could not be released by any single person without approval from a committee, and the monastery in no way wanted to be accused of participating in a coverup.

Apart from that knowledge and awareness of the stakes, however, they pleaded total ignorance about the document. They claimed that they could not confirm whether they had it or not. They blamed this on the incompleteness of their translation project of the ancient documents.

Did that make sense? Of course not.

Could they be held to account or be challenged?

Once again, of course not.

It seemed that short of an order from the Dalai Lama, their ancient manuscripts would remain where they were, untouched and un-
investigated, and the Notovitch document would never see the light of
day.

I am grasping at straws, perhaps, to say that a respected psychic I
know once claimed that Edward T. Martin's efforts and my efforts
and our film and books would have the result of "causing" the Notovitch document to suddenly "appear" one day.

I could only hope that such would be the case.

I dare not hold my breath, however.

But surely the film and the Edward T. Martin books will emphasize the point, for all to see, that the document is known to have existed and is known to be missing, and that it is wanted to answer some
of the most important questions there are about the history of religion
and the foundations of Christianity.

At that point in the production of the film, my travels were not
yet done. Anil Urmil had come in to examine my director's cut and to
begin to offer some incisive suggestions. That resulted in his coming
aboard as an editor to join me, to create the final product with me out
of what was now approaching one hundred fifty hours of material.
And we were aiming for a film just over ninety minutes in length. (The
final product was ninety-seven minutes, which Anil always said was
what he thought would be the ideal number. Then I added about eigh-
ty minutes of bonus features to the DVD.)

There were seven more specific contributions to the film by other
interviewees. One of them did not work out. The excellent German
author, Holger Kersten, whose book *Jesus Lived in India* and
other writings have contributed much to this field, sent me an interview in which he attempted to answer a list of questions I had sent to
him.

Afterwards, we both agreed that it would have been much better
if he had done the interview in his native German. He would be the
first to admit the difficulty he had with English, and none of that interview appears in the film. However, there are discussions about his
work, and he kindly provided the image of the sculpted feet of Yuz
Asaf at the Rozabal tomb in Kashmir, because my film crew was not
able to see it. The area where it was held was locked, and it was covered with a cloth so it could not be photographed.

It appears certain that someone or some group of individuals or-
ganizations has strong feelings about wanting to suppress this infor-

mation. The image in that carving clearly shows what appear to be the wounds or permanent scars of crucifixion. Why should people be prohibited from photographing it and researching its origins?

The remaining interviews were to be conducted with Suzanne Olsson (who had attempted to recover DNA samples from the remains of Yuz Asaf and Mary who is buried in Murree, Pakistan; Rabbi Yitzchok Adlerstein, professor of Jewish law at Loyola University, who could answer questions about the Jewish interpretation of the meaning of "Messiah" and methods of Jewish burial; Arif Khan, an intellectual and Ahmadiyya Muslim scholar in London who was webmaster of tombofjesus.com; Prof. James Deardorff, a former professor from Oregon State University who believed that Jesus had survived the crucifixion; Michael Hesemann, a Vatican-accredited journalist and devout Catholic who challenged whether a sufficient case had been made for Jesus having traveled to India; and perhaps most interestingly, with Monsignor Corrado Balducci, an Apostolic Nuncio of the Vatican during the time of Pope John Paul II who believed people in India had distorted the facts of Jesus' life to claim the India travel and that no documents except the canonical New Testament gospels should be used to draw any conclusions about the life of Jesus.

Suzanne Olsson's interview was filmed at her home in Florida by a local cameraman with whom I made arrangements. It was based on questions I had sent to her, since I was unable to travel to Florida at a time she could see me, and we did not want to delay the process.

Her book *Jesus in Kashmir: The Lost Tomb*, is a major contribution to this field, as are her other intriguing writings. She has had extensive experience regarding the purported Tomb of Mother Mary in Murree, Pakistan, and she placed her life in danger while doing research there. She also has extensive first-hand knowledge of the Tomb of Yuz Asaf (the Rozabal) in Srinagar. You know from the previous chapter that one of the local Muslim residents near the Rozabal spoke with vehemence about a "western lady" who tried to get a DNA sample from the remains of the prophet, and she was stopped. I knew from Suzanne Olsson's writings that the Muslim neighbor of that very ancient tomb must have been speaking about her. Getting the interview from her was an essential "missing piece" in my story, and her cooperation helped the film immeasurably.

Rabbi Yitzchok Adlerstein is a Professor of Jewish Law at Loyola University and a scholar of Judaism. When asked for an interview, he professed not to have much knowledge on our topic, but in fact he made a significant contribution. He helps viewers to understand how the expected Messiah was viewed by the Jewish population of Israel in the days of Jesus: that among other things the Messiah would unite the tribes of Israel, which had been scattered.

Groups that claim descent from specific Lost Tribes of Israel include the following: the Bene Ephraim from southern India, who claim descent from the Tribe of Ephraim; the Bnei Menashe from northeast India, who claim descent from the lost Tribe of Manasseh; the Nasranis of Malabar, India, who are of Hebrew or Israeli heritage but cannot be connected to a specific lost tribe; Ethiopian Jews who claim descent from the lost Tribe of Dan; Persian Jews who claim descent from the Tribe of Ephraim; and Igbo jews of Nigeria who claim descent from the Tribes of Levi, Zebulun, Gad, ephraim and Menasseh.

The Bene Israel, which is Hebrew for the "Sons of Israel," live in Indian cities that include Mumbai, Pune, Ahmadabad, and Karachi, which is now part of Pakistan. Other descendants of the Lost Tribes of Israel appear in various other places in Africa and Asia.

We know that the forefathers of the Kashmiri people were Jewish and from Israel. This has been proven by both DNA studies and linguistic studies. It therefore makes it not at all improbable that Jesus of Nazareth would have had reason to travel to Kashmir to make contact with the one of the Lost Tribes of Israel, especially given that the land had a rich Hebrew / Jewish heritage that included having a Temple of Solomon that replicated the Temple of Solomon in Israel. We know that Yuz Asaf appeared at that Temple of Solomon and proclaimed himself a prophet of the children of Israel (not a prophet of Egypt as the Muslims living near the Rozabal Tomb have claimed). We know from related testimony among Afghani Christians that they learned Christianity from Yuz Asaf, who told the same parables that are attributed to Christ in the New Testament, including the story of the sower.

Rabbi Adlerstein also clarified that in fact it was prevalent in the days of Jesus for Jews to bury their dead in an east-west direction, rather than north-south (which is the Muslim way of burial). Thus, the east-west orientation of the sarcophagus in the Rozabal is of significance in giving credence to the notion that Yuz Asaf was of Jewish origin.

Meeting up with Arif Khan required a trip to London, which took place early in 2006.

From Suzanne Olsson and Edward T. Martin, I had learned about Arif Khan, the young man of Ahmadiyya Muslim persuasion who was the webmaster of www.tombofjesus.com

That website had become a focal point for research about Jesus in India. As previously indicated, the Ahmadiyyas constitute a branch of Islam that has been ostracized by all other branches of the Muslim religion. They believe that the Rozabal Tomb does contain the mortal remains of Jesus of Nazareth.

However, and perhaps mysteriously, they do not believe that Jesus traveled to India in his youth during the Missing Years.

That adds up to an unusual combination of beliefs -- rejecting the youthful travel to India in the life of Christ but accepting that Jesus' life continued after the crucifixion (as they say) failed to put him to death. Many of the younger generation of Ahmadiyya Muslims, however, such as Arif Khan, are more open-minded than some of their older peers to the possibility that Jesus made both journeys to India. In fact, the website www.tombofjesus.com has certainly let its visitors know about our film and the Edward T. Martin books.

In any event, getting to have an interview with Arif Khan amounted to a golden opportunity for the film. The title I was considering, in fact, was the same as the title of a book written by Mirza Ghulam Ahmad, the founder of the Ahmadiyya movement long ago: **"Jesus in India."**

Arif Khan met with me over two days at my hotel in London and gave an extensive interview, filling in many of the missing pieces in the Jesus in India story. He was so well-educated and so eloquent, he was able to parry and thrust in precise and deft ways to provide a counterpoint to some of the pronouncements of the Catholic professors in the motion picture.

Much later, after the completion of the film, Arif Khan designed the website for our film: www.jesus-in-india-the-movie.com He married in October, 2008, and came with his bride, Rachel, to California for the public premiere of **"Jesus in India"** at the Camelot Theater in Palm Springs. He made a major contribution to the panel discussion that night, which is part of the seventy-five minutes or more of bonus materials on the DVD of **"Jesus in India."**

The interview with Professor James Deardorff was an opportunity to have a vocal religious skeptic express his point of view and his

doubts about the resurrection. Unsaid in the film is the fact that Prof.
Deardorff was a devout, practicing Protestant for most of his life. At
some point along the way, however, he began asking questions and his
former religious certainties became unraveled. He believes that Rozabal is the tomb of Jesus Christ. He believes Jesus survived the crucifixion and actually met with the Apostles afterwards. He takes the stories
in the New Testament about Jesus eating fish with the Apostles and
walking before them on the road to Galilee, after the crucifixion, quite
literally. He also takes the quotation of Jesus literally, when, after the
crucifixion and in the company of the disciples, Jesus insists that he is
not a ghost or spirit, that he is actually there in flesh and blood, and he
offers to let Doubting Thomas touch his wounds.

Prof. Deardorff believes that Jesus, alive and in his own body (not
a "resurrected" body) literally did encounter Saul of Tarsus (who became St. Paul) on the road to Damascus. He believes that Damascus is
where Jesus hid from the Romans for a time, before he headed back
to India, taking Mother Mary with him. He is a strong critic of those
who claim that Mother Mary lived in Ephesus, Turkey, after the crucifixion, and he does not believe in the literal ascension of Jesus or Mary
to heaven, or that Jesus sits at the right hand of God, or that there will
be a second coming in which Jesus returns again in the flesh.

He does, however, believe in the wisdom of Jesus, which he feels
was distorted over the years. Unlike almost every other Biblical scholar, he also believes that the Gospel of Matthew was written first, before the Gospel of Mark. He thinks that conclusion would help
resolve numerous Biblical inconsistencies (see his book ***The Problem of New Testament Gospel Origins***). He also gives credence
to a book called ***The Talmud of Jmannuel***, which claims that the
earliest gospel, that was used as a source by the other New Testament
writers for their four similar accounts of Jesus' life, was found in Jerusalem and then tragically destroyed during a raid on a Palestinian refugee camp where it was being translated. There is scant evidence,
except for the testimony of one man (who has made a series of rather
incredible claims) that the so-called ***Talmud of Jmmanuel*** ever
really did exist, although Edward T. Martin believes that Professor
Deardorff has done some very important (and under-appreciated)
Biblical research. However, claims for ***The Talmud of Jmannuel***
document certainly cannot be compared, in terms of degree of credibility, to the situation with ***The Life of St. Issa*** at the Hemis monastery, where the document was seen and translated numerous times

by a variety of scholars from different countries over a period of decades.

It was a great opportunity to have Professor Deardorff participate in the film, and he defends his views with conviction. He has written several books to coalesce those points of view.

There were two other interviews filmed in late 2005 in Italy, one with Michael Hesemann, a Vatican-accredited journalist, and the other with Monsignor Corrado Balducci.

Those took place in Lamezia, Italy. I had been invited to give a presentation about my film, **"Roswell,"** at a conference about extraterrestrial life at the University there. I conducted the two interviews while there for that conference, in which both of those men participated.

Michael Hesemann is not only a scholar on Biblical matters, who wrote a remarkable treatise on apparently successful efforts to identify part of the "real cross" of Jesus that was found in Jerusalem. It was part of the sign on the cross that declared that Jesus was "The King of the Jews." He coordinated scientific tests on the ancient piece of wood with legible writing that was unearthed during a Jerusalem construction project. His findings were personally presented to Pope John Paul II, and he wrote a book about the subject. He is a devout Catholic, but he is also a strong believer in extraterrestrial life and has long been considered an expert in the UFO field.

Michael Hesemann does not believe that Jesus traveled to India. He believes that Jesus died on the cross, and he believes in the resurrection. He has a counter-argument for every argument made by Jesus in India proponents. He appears in my film to offer some of his skepticism to the Jesus in India theory. He states quite eloquently that he has no theological objections to Christ having been in India (at least during the ages twelve to thirty). He observes that "our Lord may have traveled anywhere, and who are we to say he should not have done that?" But he states that in order to believe a part of history is true, we must examine sound and testable evidence. He does not believe the case that Jesus was in India has been won. (Although he does believe the case for the resurrection of Jesus from the dead and the ascension of Mary to heaven has been won!)

He is curious about the Nicolas Notovitch document and would like nothing more than to find it and submit it to scientific testing if it could ever be found. Until that is done, however, he feels we cannot progress much further beyond anecdotes, and the enigmatic translations of that document, a document which for reasons we do not know does not seem to exist anywhere today. And he does stand by the statements of St. John at the end of the ***Gospel of John***, that the Lord did many things that were not included in the Gospels.

Last but certainly not least, I must discuss the marvelous interview in Italian with Monsignor Corrado Balducci, who sadly passed away in September 2008, a little more than three years after my interview with him.

Although I filmed at the Vatican to be able to show its buildings and statues, the Balducci interview, like the Hesemann interview, was conducted in Lamezia, Italy.

Balducci was there to speak at the UFO conference, as he has done at so many conferences, promoting the viewpoint that belief in intelligent space alien life does not contradict Catholic theology.

This is a remarkable mission Balducci undertook during the final years of his life. He had been one of the major exorcists of the Vatican. He was also Apostolic Nuncio under John Paul II, representing the Vatican in Washington, D.C. He was in tune with the pulse and thinking of the highest levels of the Vatican throughout his life. Enigmatically, at some point, he began appearing at UFO conferences to declare that flying saucers are not illusions and that reports of space alien visitations are not to be confused with angels, demons, mirages, dreams or imaginings, at least not in all cases. He gave the oft-repeated argument that if God had created an empty universe, with life existing only upon this Earth, it would have been a waste of good real estate. He claimed that when Jesus spoke of "many mansions in His father's Kingdom," Jesus was referring to sentient life on other worlds as well as our own.

In 2008, we also saw a top Vatican astronomer declaring that belief in extraterrestrial life is not in conflict with Catholicism, and we saw a top astronaut, Edgar Mitchell, who walked on the moon longer than any other human being, declare that space aliens are here, governments of the world know it, and there has been a coverup for over sixty years.

It would appear that something is happening on that issue, that a change of thinking is arriving, and that it already has arrived at the Vatican, one of the most conservative places on Earth. After all, it was the Vatican that was among the last to accept the truth of Galileo's discovery that the Earth revolves around the sun, rather than the other way around. For centuries, "infallible" Catholicism declared that the Earth was at the center of God's creation.

As far-reaching as Monsignor Balducci's thoughts and pro-nouncements are about extraterrestrial visitation (a subject which for many people still seems to be quite "out there"), as far as Jesus in India is concerned, Balducci was perhaps the most closed-minded spokesman in the film.

Put another way, his mind was made up and there would be no persuading him otherwise. I knew this would be the case before the interview began. In fact, I was warned by author Paola Harris, an Italian friend of Balducci, that I should not even attempt to interview him about Jesus in India. "He will go ballistic!" she cautioned me.

"But why?" I asked. "He won't even discuss it?"

"The Vatican does not accept that Jesus ever went to India. What do you expect him to say? He won't want to talk about it. I'm his friend, but I wouldn't even dare bring it up."

"He'll state publicly that UFO's are real but he refuses to concede that Jesus may have traveled in India?"

"Exactly," she said.

With that warning, I took another approach. "Would he give me an interview about UFO's?" I asked. "Surely, he would do that."

"Of course you can talk to him about UFO's," said Paola Harris. "He feels it's his mission to discuss UFO's, because he does not believe that the existence of UFO's conflicts with Catholicism, and he wants people everywhere to know that."

"Well, then, please get me an interview with him about extraterrestrials and UFO's, and let me take it from there."

She rolled her eyes, knowing trouble was coming.

I'm certainly not the first documentary filmmaker who obtained an interview on a subject of my choosing under false pretenses. But I don't feel guilty about it, because even after the explosion that followed, and after the filming, Balducci signed a release permitting me to use his interview. The release was explained to him in detail by the Italian translator. I had his permission. It was in writing.

This was the way I brought it up. I began talking to him about UFO's. He explained his beliefs, that are authorized by the Vatican, that there are other intelligent sentient beings in God's universe. We are not the only ones. Some of them come here. They are not angels or devils. They are like us, people from other worlds.

I told him that I had been in India recently researching the topic of UFO's. I asked him if he believed people saw UFO's in India as well as other places.

"Of course," he said, while the camera was rolling.

"Well, I want to tell you, while I was in India, I heard the strangest thing – I had never heard anything like it before in my life. I was somewhat shocked. Did you know there are people over there in India who actually believe that Jesus visited India during his lifetime? Have you ever heard of such a thing?"

Well, that got him started.

And once he got started on the topic, he wasn't about to stop.

He stated with conviction that if there are any documents in India

Paul Davids (left) with Monsignor Corrado Balducci in Lamezia, Italy

that seem to support that claim, then they must be false documents. He believed the story was made up in India and has no foundation. It is not clear why he was unwilling even to consider the possibility. It seemed very disingenuous to me, and it does to audiences of the film, that Monsignor Balducci claimed never to have heard that there were "Missing Years" in the life of Jesus.

He stated: "This is the first time I have heard that in all my theological studies!"

But obviously that cannot be true.

So why would a man of his intelligence and stature even maintain that?

Why would he not face up to the issue of the Missing Years, or as Catholics sometimes refer to them, the "Hidden Years"?

We can only speculate. However, Brother Chidananda has pointed out that throughout the centuries the Catholic authorities have sought out and destroyed accounts that conflict with their own dogma, their own interpretations of the life of Jesus and its meaning and purpose. The church has not been immune from charges of book burning. The records of the ancient Egyptians and ancient Mayan and Aztec cultures are gone from the face of the earth, partly due to their destruction by fanatic Catholics who considered them pagan and demonic.

It is not too difficult a leap to imagine that there may be some in orthodox Christian circles who consider the Jesus in India material contrary to the interests of their own orthodoxy. Have actions been taken to seize and sequester the documents that we know exist that we are seeking? I am speaking specifically of the Notovitch document. Arguments that it never existed or was a fabrication by Notovitch are completely unpersuasive, in view of the evidence we and others have collected that it was seen by numerous reliable people over the decades.

It proved remarkable for the film to be able to juxtapose the interview with Monsignor Balducci in Italian with the interview with the Shankaracharya of Puri in Hindi. The clash of these titans provides one of the starkest contrasts and conflicts imaginable.

The foregoing account describes how I filmed and compiled the remainder of material in the film, the sections that were not filmed in India. Although no one else connected with the filming in India traveled with me for the rest of this massive amount of filming, Edward Martin (who of course was with me when I came to Texas) and Anil Urmil and others were continuing to make an invaluable contribution. In fact, the film could not have been made without them.

Anil Kumar Urmil's contribution as producer in India, and his continued contribution in the editorial process, were a major element in the making of the motion picture, and I am indebted to him for that excellent work. On my own, I had no access to the people in India who helped us. It was phenomenal that we had access to the Shanka-racharya and the high priest of Meenakshi Temple. It was also remarkable that, with help from Sanjay Shetye and Dnyanesh Moghe, we obtained access to the key personnel of the Hemis Monastery.

Principal photography continued on this film sporadically for about eight months after our return from six weeks of filming in India. Post-produduction continued for two years after my return from India.

In the final analysis, as coherent and probing as the film may be, it was the music score of Brian Thomas Lambert that was the thread that wove the whole project together, at an emotional level. Brian speaks eloquently and in detail about his composing this score as part of the Bonus Materials of the DVD of **"Jesus in India."**

This Afterword would not be complete without including mention of the editorial process. We created several versions of the film. After each version (the first of which had a running time of two hours and twenty minutes) we showed the film to a test audience. I invited their comments. When each screening was finished, I asked those who wanted to critique the film to stand, and I took notes on all of their reactions. This happened again and again, with the film undergoing changes after each screening. We were helped by specific editorial consulting by Ian Goodman, Scott Davids, Robert Rotstan, Jr., Brian Thomas Lambert and Jillian Burgin.

A lot of the work was directed toward melding Edward T. Martin's personal story into the overall search for information about Jesus in India and our journey.

Finally, when the vast majority of the test audiences were fully absorbed throughout the film and had no major requests or suggestions for changes, I decided that the film was finished.

Ric Trader at CCI was instrumental in handling the technical aspects of post-production. We were working with video material that had been filmed in numerous formats. Some was standard definition at 30 frames a second, other parts had been shot at 24 frames per second. There was PAL footage. There was high-definition. The completion process involved converting all of the formats to high-definition with a unified cadence. He also worked extensively on suitably enhancing the historic artwork photography of Jesus that appears throughout the film. Then came extensive color correction work by Greg Kibler, sound mixing with John Carter of CCI and the handling of captions and subtitles as well as opening and end credits. We worked with my daughter, Jordan Duvall, to create the Jesus in India font style and the key art. My wife, Hollace Davids, helped extensively with marketing issues.

So much of our heritage and culture is bound up in religious beliefs and the Christian story as the Bible tells it. We have been bombarded for the first decade of the new millennium with the breakdown of the wall of separation of church and state. We have lived with political leaders who believe they are not just elected by the people but appointed by God. We have leaders who believe in the Second Coming and the inevitability of Armageddon. Clearly there are severe dangers to the public interest, and dangers to mankind throughout the world, when there is a complete unwillingness to examine religious assumptions, because to do so is "heresy." And this holds true no matter what the religion, whether it be Christianity, Hinduism, Judaism, Islam or Buddhism.

Regarding Christianity, it is a jolt to many people to hear that the story of Jesus has been told in another way, with drastically different interpretations than the stories they know from having been taught about Christmas and Easter. With that in mind, just like with other controversial films I have produced, this was an uphill battle, and it still is.

It was gratifying to all involved in our film when Belinda Menendez, President of NBC Universal's International Television Distribution, decided to take on *"Jesus in India"* for worldwide distribution to broadcasters. Similarly, when Christian Vesper of the Sundance Channel picked up the film to feature in prime time on their channel at Christmas, we felt that our work would achieve impact and in time would find its way to widespread audiences, perhaps in almost every country in the world.

Author's Concluding Note

"King of Wisdom" is a phrase which is used several times in the *Talmud of Jmmanuel* which is claimed to be a translation of a document from the time of Jesus that was allegedly destroyed during military action at a refugee camp in Lebanon in 1974.

Research is greatly handicapped by the fact that this manuscript, provided it really existed, is not accessible by scholars and scientists. However, one of my close friends, Dr. James Deardorff, who is discussed several times in this book, is one of the foremost experts on this ancient text, and he in fact believes it to be the original Gospel of Matthew, or, proto-Matthew.

Dr. Deardorff's website gives the complete background of the story about this purported document. His website, which contains an intriguing amount of scholarly research, many connecting links, and the entire text of the *Talmud of Jmmanuel* is: www.tjresearch.info

Dr. Deardorff also explains that according to this information, the name Jmmanuel (spelled intentionally with a "J" at the beginning) is the real name by which Jesus was known during his life and it means "the one with Godly knowledge." I would refer the interested reader to visit that website.

Also, of related interest and relevance, I would suggest a study of the materials at the website maintained by webmaster Arif Khan:
www.tombofjesus.com

14. Bibliography

Abhedananda, Swami. *Journey into Kashmir and Tibet*. Hollywood, California: Vedanta Press, 1987.

Ahmad, Kwaja Nazir. *Jesus in Heaven on Earth*

Ahmad, Hazrat Mirza Ghulam. *Jesus in India*

Andrugtsang, Gompo Tashi. *Four Rivers, Six Ranges: Reminiscences of the Resistance Movement in Tibet*. Dharamsala, India: Information and Publicity Office of H.H. The Dalai Lama, 1973.

Bedford, Jimmy. *Around the World on a Nickel*. New Delhi, India: Vir Publishing House, 1967.

Bock, Janet. *The Jesus Mystery: Of Lost Years and Unknown Travels*. Van Nuys, California: Aura Books, 1980.

Bruknaer, Nelson T. *The Second Life of Jesus Christ*.

Bushby, Tony. *The Bible Fraud*. The Pacific Blue Group, Inc. Brisbane, Australia (2001)

Cerminara, Dr. Gina. *Many Mansions*.

Coleman, Loren. *Tom Slick and the Search for the Yeti*.

Cronk, Walter. *The Golden Light*. Santa Monica, California: DeVorss & Co., 1964.

Davidson, Art. *Minus 148 degrees: The Winter Ascent of Mt. McKinley*. New York: W.W. Norton & Co. Inc., 1969. [True story of the first winter ascent of Alaska's Mt. McKinley; Ray Genet was one of the climbers and is on the book's cover.]

Deardorff, Dr. James W. *Celestial Teachings*. Tigard, Oregon: Wild Flower Press, 1992.

Deardorff, Dr. James W. *Jesus in India: A Reexamination of Jesus' Asian Traditions in the Light of Evidence Supporting Reincarnation.* San Francisco, CA. International Scholars Publications, 1994.

Deardorff, Dr. James W. *The Problems of New Testament Gospel Origins: A Glasnost Approach.* Lewiston, New York: Edwin Mellen Press.

Deardoff, Dr. James W. *A Refutation of False Claims and Distortions by Korff.* Pamphlet. 1996.

Dowling, Levi. *The Aquarian Gospel of Jesus the Christ.* Santa Monica, California: DeVorss & Co., 1907.

Easton, Robert. *Guns, Gold, & Caravans.* Santa Barbara, California: Capra Press, 1978. [The extraordinary life and times of Fred Meyer Schroder, frontiersman and soldier of fortune in old California, Alaska, and China.]

Franck, Irene M. and David M. Brownstone. *The Silk Road: A History.* New York: Facts on File Publications, 1986.

Greiner, James, foreword by Bradford Washburn. *Wager with the Wind: The Don Sheldon Story.* New York,1974, Rand McNally & Co. [Sheldon was one of Alaska's most legendary bush pilots and he had a long association with Mt. McKinley.]

Heuvelmans, Bernard. *On The Track of Unknown Animals.* Cambridge, Massachusetts: MIT Press, 1955.

Holy Bible. King James Version. New York: Zondervan Press.

Hunter, J.A. *Hunter,* J.A. Hunter. New York: Harper & Brothers, 1952. [True story of a professional hunter in old-time East Africa.]

Isherwood, Christopher, trans. *The Bhagavad Gita.* New York: Penguin Books, 1962.

Johnson, Osa. *I Married Adventure.* New York: Garden City Publishing, 1940. [True story of pioneering wildlife photographers Martin and Osa Johnson who lived many years at Lake Paradise in Marsabit, Kenya.]

Kashmiri, Aziz. *Christ in Kashmir.* Kashmir, India: Roshni Publications, Srinagar, 1973.

Kersten, Holger. *Jesus Lived in India,* 1986, Shaftesbury, Dorset, England: Element Books, 1986.

Kinder, Gary. *Light Years.* New York: Atlantic Monthly Press, 1987.

Kinugawa, Masaaki. *Iai-Do: The Art of Japanese Swordsmanship.* Osaka, Japan: Toyoshigyo Printing Co., 1973.

Kolosimo, Peter. *Not of This World.* Seacausus, New Jersey: University Books, 1971.

Leonardi, Dell. *The Reincarnation of John Wilkes Booth: A Case Study in Hypnotic Regression.* Old Greenwich, Connecticut: Devin-Adair Co., 1975.

Mackal, Roy P. *Searching for Hidden Animals.* Garden City, New York: Doubleday and Co., 1980.

Michaud, Roland and Sabrina. *Afghanistan.* London: Thames and Hudson, 1980. [Absolutely the most dazzling and unforgettable color photographs of Afghanistan are those taken by the Michauds.]

Miyamoto, Musashi. *A Book of Five Rings: The Classic Guide to Strategy.* Kyushu, Japan: 1645. [The true story of Musashi Miyamoto, Japan's most famous and beloved folk hero/samurai.]

Notovitch, Nicolas. *The Unknown Life of Jesus Christ.* London, 1895.

Olsson, Suzanne. *Jesus in Kashmir: Jesus of Kashmir: The Lost Tomb,* 2007

Pappas, Paul C. *Jesus' Tomb in India: The Debate on His Death and Resurrection,* Berkeley, California: Asian Humanities Press, 1991.

Prophet, Elizabeth Clare. *The Lost Years of Jesus.* Livingston, Montana: Summit University Press, 1984.

Reeves, Richard. *Passage to Peshawar.* New York: Simon & Schuster, 1984.

Roerich, Nicholas, *Altai-Himalaya, A Travel Diary.* 1929.

Roy, Protap Chandra, trans. *The Mahabharata.* Calcutta: 1889.

Sasamori, Junzo. *This is Kendo: The Art of Japanese Fencing.* Rutland, Vermont: Charles E. Tuttle Co., 1964.

Service, Robert. *The Spell of the Yukon.* New York: Dodd, Mead, & Co., 1907. [Classic and charming collection of Service's poems about the Gold Rush and Far North.]

Siemel, Sasha. *Tigrero.* [Adventures of a jaguar hunter in old-time Brazil.]

Rawicz, Slavomir. *The Long Walk: A Gamble for Life.* New York: Harper & Row, 1956. [True story of a 4,000 mile walk from a Siberian prison camp to British India, including the sighting of two Yetis.]

Smith, Warren. *Strange Abominable Snowmen.* New York: Popular Library, 1970.

Snyder, Howard H. *The Hall of the Mountain King.* New York: Charles Scribner's Sons, 1973. [True story of a tragic climb of Mt. McKinley.]

Stevens, Wendelle, ed. *Messages From the Pleiades: The Contact Notes (Volumes 1-4) of Eduard Billy Meier.* Tucson, Arizona: UFO Photo Archives.

Stevens, Wendelle, ed. *UFO Contact From the Pleiades.* Munds Park, Arizona: Genesis III Publishing, 1980.

Thomas, Lowell. *Good Evening Everybody: From Cripple Creek to Samarkand.* New York: Avon Books, 1976.

Valli, Eric and Diane Summers. *Honey Hunters of Nepal.* New York: Harry N. Abrams Inc. Publishers, 1988.

Winters, Randolph. *The Pleiadian Mission: A Time of Awareness.* Rancho Mirage, California:The Pleiades Project, 1994.

Yogananda, Paramahansa. *The Second Coming of Christ: The Resurrection of the Christ Within You.* (Two Volumes) Los Angeles, California. Self-Realization Fellowship, 2007

Ziegler, Julie H., trans. *The Talmud of Jmmanuel.* Tigard, Oregon: Wild Flower Press, 1992.

About the Author

Edward T. Martin was raised in the small town of Lampasas in central Texas. During his childhood, on summer vacation trips with his parents, he was able to visit many parts of the United States.

At the age of nineteen, he drove with a friend to Alaska to fight summer forest fires with the Bureau of Land Management. He attended the University of Alaska at Fairbanks, where he later graduated with a Bachelor of Arts degree in Speech Communications. At the age of twenty-one, he made his first overseas trip to Kenya, Tanzania (where he climbed to the summit of Mt. Kilimanjaro) and Uganda. While in Alaska, he was actively involved with parachuting, archery and mountaineering (including a summit climb of Mt. McKinley).

After graduating from UAF, he became a Peace Corps volunteer, teaching English as a Second Language (ESL) in Afghanistan. While in Asia, he traveled extensively in Afghanistan, Pakistan, India and Nepal. During his travels in India, he researched the subject of Jesus in India and found a surprising amount of historical evidence and folklore.

Later, he was a Peace Corps volunteer for two years in the South Pacific, in the Fiji Islands. During that time, he traveled extensively in Fiji, New Zealand and Australia. After leaving Fiji, he lived for one year at Izumo, Japan where he taught ESL and studied the martial arts of Kendo and Iaido (Fencing and Swordsmanship), earning a Shodan degree in both.

He also taught ESL for one year at Taif, Saudi Arabia for Siyanco Corporation and later he taught ESL to Afghan refugees at Peshawar, Pakistan. In the United States he has worked as a teacher, a newspaper reporter and photographer and as the manager of a publishing company. He is an avid student of comparative religion, spirituality, history and foreign cultures. A gifted linguist, he speaks seven languages.

While living in Austin, Texas, he established Jonah Publishing, which published the first edition of ***King of Travelers: Jesus' Lost Years in India***. The two printings of that edition sold out.

In 2005, Edward T. Martin embarked with Hollywood producer / director / writer Paul Davids on the filming of the feature-length documentary motion picture, **"Jesus in India**." The film was years in the making, involving six weeks of shooting in India at forty locations. Filming took place in a total of four countries (India, England, Italy and the United States) and at six locations in the United States (Los Angeles; Texas; Washington, D.C.; Princeton, New Jersey; New York City and Amherst, Massachusetts). Edward T. Martin appears in the film, which is based upon his research, and he is credited as associate producer.

During post-production on **"Jesus in India,"** the Author moved from Austin to Tucson, Arizona, where he works on the TV series **"The Cutting Edge"** and teaches English as a second language. In Tucson, he completed writing this book that he began in India while the motion picture expedition there was underway.

Mr. Martin is also available for public speaking, conferences, and workshops about Jesus in India and related topics.

In 2008, the motion picture **"Jesus in India,"** was picked up for international television distribution by NBC Universal's division known as Universal City Studios Productions, LLLC, which is part of Universal's International Television Distribution. NBC Universal, in turn, has arranged for broadcast of the film on The Sundance Channel and licenses it to television all around the world.

A Widescreen DVD Special Edition of the 97 minute feature film with about 80 minutes of Bonus Features, released by Yellow Hat Productions, Inc. in conjunction with the Sundance Channel broadcasts, can be ordered at the website for the film as well as other vendors:

www.jesus-in-india-the-movie.com

Edward T. Martin may be contacted by email at

jonahpublishing23@hotmail.com

or info@jesus-in-india-the-movie.com

About the Motion Picture

The DVD of "**Jesus in India**" is available at www.jesus-in-india-the-movie.com

It's a widescreen special edition with the 97 minute documentary feature film and about 80 minutes additional Bonus Materials. The additional materials include Edward T. Martin on "**The Cutting Edge**" TV show. There are also in-depth commentaries that were filmed at the Film Forecast Conference at Big Bear Lake, California in June, 2008. Producer / Director / Editor Paul Davids appeared at the conference with fellow producer-editor Anil Kumar Urmil, along with Assistant Director Nelvan Thomas Binny of Mumbai, India. Composer Brian Thomas Lambert also appeared. Also included is a panel discussion at the first public showing of "**Jesus in India**" at the Camelot Theater in Palm Springs on October 21, 2008. Present and participating were Paul Davids, Arif Khan, Sanjay Shetye, Brian Lambert, Robert Rotstan, Jr. and Edward T. Martin. Additionally, the Bonus Materials include an extended interview with Princeton Professor of Religion and noted author Elaine Pagels; the trailer for the feature film; Paul Davids speaking about his background in television and film, and a gallery of photographs with music excerpts from Brian Thomas Lambert's score of the motion picture.

The CD of the entire soundtrack music score of the film is also available at the website of the film.

Noted critic Pete Hammond of Hollywood.com states that "'**Jesus in India**' is a fascinating and profound film, a deeply spiritual journey certain to make you think and question in ways you never have before."

You can learn more about the film's director, Paul Davids, and previous films he has made and books he has written at www.pauldavids.com

www.jesus-in-india-the-movie.com

You will want to read the new edition of the companion book to this one, the revised and updated version of the book that inspired the motion picture of "Jesus in India." It is also by Edward T. Martin: *King of Travelers: Jesus' Lost Years in India*:

To order *King of Travelers: Jesus' Lost Years in India* or the DVD of **"Jesus in India"** or the CD of the Music Soundtrack of the film go to www.jesus-in-india-the-movie.com

Printed in the United States of America